YOU KNOW YOUR LIFE IS A SOAP OPERA IF...

HYPERION
New York

YOU KNOW YOUR LIFE IS A SOAP OPERA IF...

gerry waggett

Printed in the United States of America. For information address Hyperion, 77 West 66th Street, New York, New York 10023-6298.

ISBN-10: 1-4013-0292-0
ISBN-13: 978-1-4013-0292-4

Hyperion books are available for special promotions and premiums. For details contact Michael Rentas, Assistant Director, Inventory Operations, Hyperion, 77 West 66th Street, 12th floor, New York, New York 10023, or call 212-456-0133.

FIRST EDITION

10 9 8 7 6 5 4 3 2 1

for

Mackey Crowley

whose prayers

helped so much

acknowledgments

My first debt of gratitude belongs to my editor, Gretchen Young, who thought of me for this project. Although we have been working together for over ten years on different books, communicating by phone and e-mail, we have never met face-to-face. I never even knew what she looked like until I saw her playing herself on *One Life to Live* last year, which further blurred for me the line between real life and daytime. Gretchen, you are always a pleasure to work with.

I would also like to thank Deborah Blackwell, executive vice president and general manager of SOAPnet, for believing in me, as well as making our phone meetings as much fun as writing the book.

For taking care of so many of the business details

surrounding this book, I thank Ruth Curry and Sarah Mandell.

On a personal note, I must thank my parents, Barbara and Fred Waggett, for their continued support throughout the years. For their contributions to my career I also need to thank my aunt Margaret Connolly; my uncle Ed Connolly; my brothers Michael, Kevin, and Freddie; my nieces Taylor, Ava, and Norma; my nephew Matthew; my sister-in-law Christine; and my cousin Mabel.

In addition to my family, my friends have played pivotal roles not only in my life but in my career: Chris Farrell, who finds me funny even when I'm not trying; Jerry Stonehouse; Jim McCarthy; Robin DiCarlo; Jim and Christina Burke and Brady; the Walshes (Jamie, Mike, Connie, Brigitte, Brendan, and Marita); George and Stacey Hrabushi, who reminded me that it's all right to pray for a book deal; JT Ahern, who inspired me during all the important homestretch; Scott Reedy; Don Casali; Mike Dubson; Dr. John Ferrante, who pushed me to stay healthy even during crunch times; Lynda Hirsch; Joanna Hussey; Steve McGee; Amanda Richards; Katie Brown and her staff at the Adams Street Library (Ed, Val, Karen, and Elissa) for providing me not only with an air-conditioned place to write, but genuine interest in my book; and Louise Schaffer, who took the time to read sections of my book while battling deadlines of her own.

I would also like to single out five teachers I've had throughout high school, college, and grad school, who really pushed me to be a better writer: Bill Collins, Kevin Kynock, Father Lawrence Corcoran, Chris Leland, and Lee Grove.

YOU KNOW
YOUR LIFE IS
A SOAP OPERA
IF...

YOU KNOW YOUR LIFE IS A SOAP OPERA IF . . .

- ✓ You are less than ten years older than your firstborn child, who is two years younger than his baby brother.
- ✓ Upon entering a room, you have ever been announced with the phrase, "The role of [your name] is now being played by . . ."
- ✓ Thoughts that should remain safely inside your head come spilling out in monologues that can be clearly overheard by anyone passing by.
- ✓ By a convoluted pattern of marriages and adoptions, you have become your own niece.
- ✓ The worst calamities always happen to your family every Friday afternoon at five minutes to four.

introduction

When I first began watching soaps in the late 1970s, ABC used to air these *F.Y.I. (For Your Information)* public service segments between each of its shows. The segments were hosted by *Barney Miller*'s Hal Linden, himself a soap vet (*Search for Tomorrow*). During the minute or two that each *F.Y.I.* ran, Hal would praise the health benefits of power-walking or advise us to stretch not only before exercising but afterward, as well. He showed us how to relieve eye strain with deep breathing and toothache pain with an ice cube placed between the thumb and index finger. All helpful hints, some of which I've followed, but to me, *F.Y.I.* felt like *Schoolhouse Rock*! for adults, a little education mixed in with the afternoon's entertainment.

At the time and to this day, I have always found the soaps an educational experience in and of themselves. In college, this rationale helped me justify skipping afternoon Shakespeare seminars to stay back in my dorm room and watch *All My Children*. I knew enough Shakespeare . . . well, enough to recognize the *Romeo and Juliet* undertones throughout each soap's teen romance.

When I talk about soaps being educational, I am not just talking about the socially relevant story lines that were coming into vogue during this time. I am talking

> "Sometimes we learned what to do by following the leading man's example; sometimes we learned what never to do by watching a vixen's scheme blow up in her face."

about the lessons that soaps were teaching without really trying—lessons about dating, maneuvering your way through big business, tricking murderers into confessing on tape, and surviving everything from divorce to flash floods. Sometimes we learned what to do by following the leading man's example; sometimes we learned what never to do by watching a vixen's scheme blow up in her face.

This book collects together some of the varied lessons I've picked up from decades of soap viewing. To start, I've compiled the ten most important lessons I myself have learned from my past twenty-odd years as a soap fan:

1. There is no such thing as a happy ending. As long as the story continues, so do the complications.

2. Everyone has a double, and more often than not, they are looking to take over your life.

3. Pregnancy, fake pregnancy, that codicil to your rich grandfather's will . . . There are many ways to trap a man into marriage, but none to trap him into a happy one.

4. Your MBA from Harvard isn't half as valuable as your birth certificate in a family business.
5. A coma is no excuse for bad hair and makeup.
6. After sex, the bedsheets need to be tucked all the way up to a woman's shoulders, but only up to a man's waist.
7. Paying blackmail never prevents the truth from coming out; it only delays the inevitable—and you don't get your money back.
8. That guy you've woken up next to after a night of heavy drinking . . . he's either dead or your new husband.
9. Whatever you think you've gotten away with . . . someone was watching.
10. Before you utter one incriminating syllable, check to see who's lurking at the window, outside the door, under the bed, and behind the drapes. Depending upon the severity of your sin and/or crime, you may want to sweep the room for listening devices.

YOU MIGHT BE LIVING IN A SOAP TOWN IF . . .

✓ No two residents have the same first name.

✓ You are an hour by train from New York City, but less than an hour's plane ride from Paris (a direct flight, mind you, from your town's international airport).

✓ Your secret-agent population is second only to that of Washington, DC.

✓ None of the residents ever knew what state the town was located in until the mid-1980s.

✓ A mad scientist has ever tried to freeze the entire town.

rediscovering the lost art of conversation

In this technological era of cell phones, text messaging, and e-mail, we are losing the all-important art of conversation. Only on the soaps do we see people who still value the face-to-face conversation, people who realize that a thousand emoticons cannot replace one arched eyebrow.

If you want to lead a soapier life, you need to start with how—and where—to conduct a successful conversation. A successful conversation, by the way, is defined as one that ends with the line, "How dare you walk into my house and say these things?"

Nothing of importance should ever be discussed on

the telephone. And not because what you say can be taped. That would actually give the phone conversation a legitimate purpose.

The telephone serves only three purposes:

1. Leaving the police anonymous tips where to find evidence you've planted.

2. Telling your blackmail victims where to drop the money off.

3. Ordering people to come to you. "Meet me in the hotel lobby in twenty minutes," you say and hang up, with no "Good-bye." If the person asked, "Who is this?," you didn't hear them. Not that you would have answered. You have already said all you intended to on a telephone. Even if the person didn't recognize your voice, they will respect your authoritative tone and get themselves over to that hotel lobby.

   (Note: Should you ever find yourself on the receiving end of such a call, as soon as you show up, you have to say, "I don't appreciate being summoned.")

Should you decide to pay a visit to someone's house, just show up at the door. Never call first. This is so important that it bears repeating: Never call before showing up. If you do, you won't catch people who shouldn't be there. You won't spy who's sneaking out in the morning, dressed in last night's tuxedo.

The unexpected knock adds a nice moment of intrigue to your host's day. "Who could that be at this time of day (or night)?" your host will remark before opening the door.

Before you ring a bell, try the knob. If the door is unlocked, then walk right in. You will overhear far more important information this way than if you're waiting in the foyer until the butler has announced you. Time your entrance for a pivotal moment in a private conversation that you can interrupt with a barb of your trademark sarcasm. Then throw yourself into the argument quickly and forcefully, before anyone thinks to ask how you got in.

Maybe it's not your style to just walk into someone's house uninvited. Until you overcome that hang-up, ring the doorbell first, wait a minute, then try the knob. If the door is open, you should feel free to walk right in. An unlocked door that no one is answering signals potential danger. Someone might be hurt or murdered inside.

If the door isn't open, don't immediately jump to the

> "If the door is unlocked, then walk right in. You will overhear far more important information this way than if you're waiting in the foyer until the butler has announced you."

conclusion that no one is home. Walk around the house, peeping in all the windows, till you spot signs of trouble.

Psychologists recommend leaving an arm's length between yourself and the person to whom you're speaking. Personal space, they call this. But that will never work for you. During the conversation, either stand right up in your host's face or on the other side of the room. That way, when one of your comments finally pushes her over the edge, you're either too far away to slap or too close for her to work up the momentum for it to hurt.

Again, despite what psychologists advocate, you do

not need to conduct conversations face-to-face. In fact, most of the successful conversations you'll ever have will be talking to the back of someone's head. While you would kill to see your host's face while you say what you've come to say, you'll know that you've hit a nerve when she finally turns around.

"Good-bye" is just as unacceptable a way to end a face-to-face (or more accurately face-to-back-of-head) meeting as it is to end a phone call. Acceptable variations on good-bye include:

- "Get out."
- "You think about what I've said."
- "Get out before I have you thrown out."
- "I'll see myself out."
- "Get out before I call the police."
- "I'll expect your answer by tomorrow."
- You, smirking.
- Your host throwing her drink against the door.

designing your dream house

Ideally, you want to move into one of the preexisting mansions in your town, perhaps the same one where your mother worked as a maid. Old houses come with a wonderful history all their own. You won't find skeletons behind any walls or treasures buried in the basement of a house you build yourself.

If you cannot buy or marry your way into one of these old homes, then pick a good location. Mansions should sit on top of a hill, where everyone in town can look up at them and wish they were you. You can also buy an island right off the coast, where everyone can look out across the water and wish they were you.

But if you do need to build a home from the ground up, bear in mind that a soap mansion is more than a big house with columns out front and a fancy name over the gate. (Speaking of names, put at least as much effort into naming your estate as you did into picking names for your children.) You need to sit down with the architect (over drinks at his place, perhaps) and explain to him your specific needs:

multiple bedrooms

It doesn't matter that you don't get along with your husband's family. It doesn't matter that every single member of that family can easily afford a mansion of their own. Once you move into a big house, your husband's entire family follows.

the forbidden wing

A mansion needs to be big enough not only to house your extended family and occasional long-term guests, but to include a sealed-off wing that no one is allowed to enter. No one. Despite the fact that your husband owns oil wells, you will maintain that the wing has proven too expensive to heat. Such a flimsy excuse will generate suspicions about "the real reason" the wing is off-limits.

secret passageways

Walking in the front door of your house becomes rather mundane very quickly. You will never tire of slipping in and out undetected via a system of secret passageways and underground tunnels.

the secret room

A home should reflect the personality of its owners. A family with as many secrets as yours should have a house with secrets of its own, like the aforementioned passageways and at least one secret room. Such rooms tend to be hidden behind bookcases, grandfather clocks, or full-length portraits, all the sorts of upscale furnishings your home should be decorated with anyway.

the fireplace

On a rainy night, when the storm has flooded the road back to town, nothing sets the stage for seduction better

“Walking in the front door of your house becomes rather mundane very quickly. You will never tire of slipping in and out undetected via a system of secret passageways and underground tunnels.”

than a roaring fire, especially one that you have asked your husband's business partner to start—after insisting that he get out of those wet clothes immediately. The fireplace will also prove indispensable for destroying evidence. So plan ahead. The size of your fireplace should be determined by how much evidence you foresee yourself needing burned at one time.

the wine cellar

In vino veritas. English translation: A couple's true feelings for one another will emerge when they are locked together in a wine cellar overnight.

the attic

You need a really spacious attic where you can store all the things that are no longer being used: old clothes, excess furniture, fur coats during the summer, and your husband's catatonic first wife.

french doors

On a warm summer day, opening up the French doors lets in the sunshine, fresh air, and all sorts of unwelcome visitors who know better than to walk up and ring the bell. Nothing sparks up an otherwise lazy afternoon like finding your worst enemy sitting on the living room sofa.

walk-in closets

You are not just a passionate lover, you are a very compassionate one as well. When your workaholic husband pops home in the middle of the afternoon, you want someplace roomy for your lover to hide.

mahogany floors

From a practical standpoint, mahogany hides a bloodstain better than ash or pine.

some help with the help

Let's face it—you didn't marry your way into that mansion on the hill to scrub the floors in all thirty-five rooms. Finding the right help can be a daunting task. You need to be even more discerning about whom you let in through the back door as servants than about whom you invite in through the front door as guests.

the butler

The sort of butler you want anticipates your every need. He can be called upon at any hour of the day or night, no matter what the reason. Even when awakened at three in the morning because you can't find your fur coat, he will not only locate it for you but help you into it, never asking any questions about where you are headed at this time of night. A butler like that will last maybe a week with the family of self-centered lunatics you've married into. Instead, you'll have to settle for that butler's rude upstart of a nephew, the one who's capricious with regards to his duties around the house. When your father-in-law asks why this man, who refuses to mix him a proper martini, has not yet been fired for insubordination, just remind him that no one else will put up with the lot of you.

the live-in maid

Candidate #1 is a beautiful young woman. Just so you know, she will not be walking around your house in a maid's uniform to put herself through nursing school. She's after your rich husband. When you pause for a moment to consider how you landed this latest millionaire of yours (who was also married at the time), you'll realize that this young lady presents way too great a threat to your marriage for you to help her with the job.

Candidate #2 has children who will be living in the servants' quarters with her. Bear in mind, kids who grow up in a big mansion like yours, even the ones who grow up in the servants' quarters, don't quite comprehend the distinction between the classes. They wind up playing with your children, and the next thing you know, your son wants to bring the maid's daughter to your black-tie fund-raiser. How long after that before he's talking marriage? Another risk of hiring mothers: If the woman happens to die on the job (on the way home from picking you up a pregnancy test, for example), the obligation to raise her children falls upon your shoulders.

Go with Candidate #3, the unmarried, middle-aged former army officer. Sure, she'll be bossing everyone around, including you, but anyone who can put your snotty sister-in-law in her place deserves the job.

the personal assistant

There's a reason she excels at dictation and has been so diligent about emptying the waste basket: She's an undercover reporter writing an exposé about your husband.

the cook

A great chef, like a great artist, is bound to be rather temperamental. Be prepared to cede control of the kitchen—a small sacrifice for you—to your cook, who will always be addressed as "Cook," no matter what his or her real name may be. Never enter the kitchen without permission or you'll be ordering pizzas for Thanksgiving dinner.

the nanny

This woman is one of the most important people you will be bringing into the house—and one of the most

> "When you do finally cross the line with your teenaged gardener, be discreet. The ladder he uses to prune the hedges should not always be propped up to your bedroom window."

dangerous. She will be caring for your baby for all but the fifteen minutes of each day when you visit the nursery to revel in the joys of motherhood. In choosing the nanny, just bear one thing in mind: The more qualified and nurturing she comes across during the interview, the more likely it is that she will be kidnapping the child at some point. She may be out for some quick ransom money, but more than likely she will be taking your baby because she can't have one of her own.

the private nurse

Triple check all her references, then hire a detective to do a complete background investigation. Specifically, you're interested in how many of her patients have died under suspicious circumstances. On second thought, maybe you're not so concerned about your mother-in-law joining that list.

the chauffeur

You may be the one he's driving all over town, but he works for your husband. Every day, he's writing reports on where you've gone and whom you're meeting. So you may want to drive yourself over to your boyfriend's apartment house for those afternoon trysts. But make no mistake. You do need a chauffeur. The way you leave restaurants, dinner parties, and board meetings ready to explode, you have no business getting behind the wheel of a car. You're almost as dangerous to yourself as those people trying to run your limo off the road.

the groundskeeper

Yes, you hate the disapproving looks he gives you, staring into the back of your limo like you don't belong here. Get used to it. The groundskeeper comes with the house. Your husband can't fire him because he knows every little secret about the family history, every sin and crime that's ever been committed on the property. He's probably dug one or two of the graves himself.

the gardener

The groundskeeper can mow the lawn and weed the garden. You're hiring this particular kid because you want to spend the summer looking at some shirtless seventeen-year-old working up a sweat in your backyard. (Since you don't have any horses on your property, it would be really suspicious for you to hire a stable boy.) When you do finally cross the line with your teenaged gardener, be discreet. The ladder he uses to prune the hedges should not always be propped up to your bedroom window. And you can't have him coming by every afternoon. Seriously, how fast do you think grass grows?

the laundress

Your first and most important question during the interview process should be, "How good are you at getting blood out?" If, as your husband suspects, you've hired that teenaged gardener for more than his green thumb, you may also want to inquire into her proficiency with grass stains.

staples for your jewelry box

No jewelry box worth its false bottom would be complete without the following . . .

- A handful of used wedding bands, each one inscribed with words like "eternal love," "always," and "forever."
- One brand new gold ring ready and waiting for your next unplanned (the unromantic may call it "impetuous") wedding.
- One lone ruby earring, the mate to which is owned by your long-lost identical twin.

- A pocket watch that belonged to your first and greatest love, the hour and minute hands frozen on that moment in time when his plane crashed and he was lost to you forever.

- The ring with the secret compartment, perfect for discreetly drugging any drink.

- The antique locket containing a photo of the baby you were forced to give away at birth. (In lieu of a photograph, the locket may contain a lock of the baby's hair, essential for the DNA test.)

- The oversized brooch with the cleverly hidden microphone inside, perfect for recording whatever drunken confessions you'll need to use against your husband during the divorce.

- Cuff links for when you go out masquerading as a man.

- A few gold bracelets you can hock to pay this month's blackmail.

we interrupt this book to bring you the following weather advisory

Soap towns suffer like no others from extreme weather conditions. Even the most landlocked lie in the path of vicious hurricanes. During the summers, temperatures often climb to the point where none of the young men can bear to walk around with their shirts on. The inhabitants of such towns have found effective methods for surviving the most brutal weather conditions.

When caught in the middle of a rainstorm . . .

> . . . the most important thing to do is find a nice dry barn where you can make love in the hayloft.

When caught in a blizzard . . .

. . . the most important thing to do is to break into a nice cabin, where you can start a fire and make love.

When the temperature drops below freezing and your car won't start . . .

. . . the most important thing to do is to take off your clothes, climb under a thick blanket, and make love.

During a heat wave . . .

. . . the most important thing to do is to find an air-conditioned pool house where you can make love.

When a tornado strikes . . .

. . . the most important thing to do is head for the basement and make love.

When caught in an avalanche . . .

. . . the most important thing to do is find a cave where you can build a fire and make love.

The soap book will now be joined in progress . . .

YOU KNOW YOU'RE A SOAP BRIDE IF YOUR GROOM AND EX-HUSBAND ARE NOT JUST BROTHERS . . .

- ✓ They are twins, identical twins.
- ✓ They are also your ex-sons-in-law.
- ✓ They are actually half brothers but won't find out until the reception this afternoon.
- ✓ They're both in love with your sister.
- ✓ They are in fact the same man, one posing as the other to win you back.

planning your wedding

If that incredibly handsome, incredibly rich man of your dreams had fallen for your jealousy games, you wouldn't have needed to fake this pregnancy to squeeze a marriage proposal out of him. But now that you have, you can start planning this month's wedding of the century.

One tip before you begin: The size and grandeur of the wedding does not determine the happiness or longevity of the marriage. So skip the horse-drawn carriage and put that money aside for marriage counseling down the line.

The first thing you need to do is pick a date. Bear in mind that there are millions of couples looking to get married each year and only 365 days to choose from. So, no matter how super a supercouple you may be, you can't have a day all to yourselves. The best you can do is pick a day when neither one of you has gotten married to anyone else.

Some superstitions are to be honored. It is considered bad luck, for example, for the groom to see the bride's wedding dress—especially on the floor outside the best man's hotel room.

There's a reason why the minister no longer asks if anyone has any objections. That whole "speak now or forever hold your peace" edict just invites trouble. If someone is hell-bent on interrupting the ceremony, she won't need to be asked.

You have a right to be suspicious of your groom if he is not inviting a single family member or any friends from his old neighborhood—wherever that may be. You might want to start your own wedding tradition: the background check.

Since you'll be taking a blood test to get your marriage license anyway, why not have your doctor compare your fiancé's DNA to your own, just to make sure that you're not marrying your own brother?

If the wedding dress comes down to a choice of two, buy both and plan on wearing the one you like just a

"Okay, the church burned down, the cake exploded, and your father was arrested for embezzlement while walking you down the aisle . . . Stop crying like this is the only wedding you're ever going to have."

little bit less to the church. Statistically speaking, this wedding won't actually be taking place today. Either your future mother-in-law or your groom's ex will be interrupting the ceremony with the results from your actual pregnancy test. This way, you will still have the nicer dress for the next wedding, which, again statistically speaking, more than likely will end with a successful exchange of vows.

Don't buy too thick a veil. You don't want any obsessed lunatics sneaking in and marrying your groom before he sees whose hand he has just taken in marriage.

More weddings might go off as planned if the modern best man worried less about finding the right strippers for the bachelor party and paid more attention to his real duties, like keeping the bride from being kidnapped.

When choosing a maid of honor, remember, you're not just finding someone to help you into your wedding dress, you're picking your husband's first mistress.

Your sinfully rich husband will probably send his lawyer over with a prenuptial agreement on the morning of the wedding. As miffed as you will be at your husband springing this on you at the last minute, sign the stupid paper. You will have the entire honeymoon to convince him to shred the agreement.

On the guest list, you need to include someone with connections to the music business. That way, in lieu of a toaster oven, they can pull a few strings to get a big-time music act, a Mary J. Blige or an Il Divo, to perform at your reception. Ideally, you'd love to have the same singer or group that recorded your theme song.

Okay, the church burned down, the cake exploded, and your father was arrested for embezzlement while walking you down the aisle . . . Stop crying like this is the only wedding you're ever going to have.

> "That whole "speak now or forever hold your peace" edict just invites trouble. If someone is hell-bent on interrupting the ceremony, she won't need to be asked."

second wedding etiquette

Divorce seldom marks the end of the road for a true supercouple like yourselves. If anything, it's par for the course, just slightly more dramatic than all the breakups you went through while dating. A lesser couple would simply slip off to a justice of the peace to retie this particular knot, but you believe that your reunion calls for another celebration throughout the land. Here you will find the answers to the most frequently asked questions facing today's second-time brides.

Should the second wedding be more or less elaborate than the first?

More elaborate than flying all your friends and family to England for a ceremony in Westminster Abbey?

More elaborate than the fireworks display afterward? More elaborate than leaving the reception in a hot-air balloon? Is that possible? For practicality if not economic reasons, couples of the marryin' kind should alternate weddings. If the first was a grand affair, keep the second one simple, immediate family down by the gazebo. This will cleanse the guests' palates for your spectacular third wedding.

What color should I wear this time around?

Anything but white, but that's what you're going to pick because you see this wedding as a new beginning. Brides don't normally get self-conscious wearing white until their third trip to the altar.

Am I allowed to wear the same engagement ring and wedding band?

Only if you can find them at the bottom of whatever lake you threw them in.

Is my fiancé allowed to have the same best man?

Unless he's been sleeping with you between the two weddings.

Should we write new wedding vows?

Absolutely. And this time, try writing ones you can keep.

Should guests bring a gift to the second wedding?

Unless the gifts from the first wedding were returned, invitations to the second should read: "No presents." Family and friends getting dressed up

> "A lesser couple would simply slip off to a justice of the peace to retie this particular knot, but you believe that your reunion calls for another celebration throughout the land."

and coming to the church all over again without taking bets on how long this go-round will last should be gift enough.

Which day should we celebrate our anniversary on? The date of the original wedding or the latest one?

This works under the presumption that this marriage will be lasting through an entire calendar year. Should you defy the historical precedent you've set, logic would dictate that you should be celebrating the anniversary of the wedding you haven't screwed up yet.

Retying the knot sounds very romantic. But getting divorced twice and then remarried for a third time may look a tad silly to some. Is there some limit on the number of times we can marry each other?

No, but there should be. When granting a couple's second petition for divorce, the judge should also be issuing a mutual restraining order to keep them away from one another from this day forward.

as long as you're going to crash the wedding . . .

Sadly, you will not be invited to every wedding in town. The only reason guards have not been hired to keep you out? No one thinks you have the audacity to show up to a wedding uninvited. They obviously don't know you too well. Since you're going to crash this wedding, you might as well . . .

object!

Just be prepared that doing so will most definitely make you *persona non grata* at the reception (not that you were invited to that, either). If, however, your objection can be backed up with those pictures in your purse, *no one* will be going to this reception.

bring the bride's ex as your guest

You would not attend a wedding you were invited to alone. Neither should you crash one alone. And who better to escort you than the one person less welcome than yourself?

kidnap the groom

The bride and groom have trod a tempestuous road to this day. When he isn't waiting on the altar for her, she won't think *kidnapped*. She'll just assume that he's jilted her yet again. While she curses him for being a coward and running out without a word of explanation, you'll have a two-day head start to spirit the groom up to a secluded mountain cabin for your own private wedding ceremony.

wear white

Etiquette books consider it extremely bad form for anyone but the bride to be wearing white. When the bride comments on your lack of taste, point out that she has no more right to be wearing white today than you do.

offer your own toast

After the best man has finished his toast, grab the microphone and add your own. Congratulate the groom on finding such a lovely bride and then, almost as an afterthought, congratulate him on his impending fatherhood with another woman.

dedicate a song to the groom

Back when you and the groom were a couple, the two of you had your own special songs, just like he has now with what's-her-veil. Request that the band dedicate a song to the groom, the same song that was playing the first time you and he ever made love. Oh, he remembers that night just as clearly and as fondly as you. If the band will allow you to join them, get up and sing the song directly to him. If you haven't been blessed with a singing voice, then just pull the groom onto the floor for a close and steamy twirl that will make that first dance with his bride look like the Hokey Pokey.

stumble in drunk

Your daughter didn't want you at her wedding because, with this whole drunken downward spiral you've been on, she was afraid that you'd embarrass her and ruin the day. So why let her down? You don't need to stay long, just long enough to help yourself to a glass of champagne or four. If you can knock over the wedding cake on your way out, that will just be the icing on it.

catch the bouquet

If you really want to surprise the bride, stay in hiding until it's time for her to toss the bouquet. Imagine the look of surprise on her face when she turns around and sees you of all people standing there, holding her flowers.

curse the bride and groom

You don't have to interrupt the wedding or the reception and make a big scene. While the newlyweds are cutting the cake, you can stand a respectful distance away and spew your venom: "I curse you. I curse you both!"

advantages of a church wedding

At least one wedding in a woman's life should take place in a church. Even if you and your groom never get to exchange "I dos," you should get that walk down the aisle. Yes, you do need to get married quickly before your fiancé finds out the truth about all your lies and schemes, and a justice of the peace would be quicker, but a church offers too many amenities that no other venue can match.

stained-glass windows

If your ex-boyfriend is inclined to literally crash the wedding, he can ride his motorcycle right through one of those huge stained-glass windows. Let's see him try to fit so much as the front tire through one of those undersized windows at City Hall.

chandeliers

Not only do chandeliers cast the perfect lighting for an evening wedding, the bolts can be loosened an hour beforehand so that one can come crashing down midceremony.

candles

Anyone wishing to stop your wedding can either light a candle and pray for a miracle or make their own miracle, tossing one of the already lit candles onto the carpet.

the choir loft

A hit man could not design a better perch for himself. From the choir loft, he has a clear shot at either you or your police detective groom. (It would be the ultimate faux pas for him to be shooting anyone else at your wedding.)

columns

Anyone wishing to slip into the church and spy on your wedding unobserved can do so very comfortably from behind one of the many columns. The bigger the church, the wider the columns. Ideally, you should choose a church big enough so that its columns can hide your groom's seven-months-pregnant ex-girlfriend.

nuns

No one is going to think twice about nuns walking around a church. So if someone were not welcome at your wedding—if security guards had been hired for the sole purpose of keeping that one person away—then dressing up as a nun would make an excellent disguise for slipping in without incident. No one, but no one, not even mob bodyguards, will mess with a nun. Habits, it should be noted, make an excellent disguise for men and women alike.

YOU KNOW YOU'RE CARRYING A SOAP BABY IF . . .

- ✓ Your best friend thinks that the child is biologically hers.
- ✓ You'll inherit $300 million if you can give birth before midnight New Year's Eve.
- ✓ You're not due for another six months, and already more than three people have filed petitions for sole custody.
- ✓ You wouldn't have gotten pregnant had your fatherhood-obsessed husband not been secretly replacing your birth control pills with placebos.
- ✓ Your granddaughter has reached her own child-bearing years.

a little help getting pregnant

Although obstetricians rarely recommend infidelity as a treatment for infertility, a one-night stand with an unsuitable partner (like your husband's black-sheep brother) will significantly increase your odds of conception.

If the black-sheep brother has already been banished to another town, you should seek out the leading cads and crime lords within your town. For some reason (maybe a testosterone overload), villains tend to be far more prolific than the average male.

Your husband does not need to waste any of his time taking fertility tests. He can have kids. He's had at least one already. Even if he doesn't know exactly which of his exes he's gotten pregnant, he can be sure that at least one of them was in the family way when he dumped her.

After your miscarriage (see "Dangers for Pregnant Women to Avoid"), your gynecologist told you that you will never have children. What he meant by this was that you wouldn't have them for at least a year or two. You can expect not only to get pregnant again but to give birth to your little miracle baby on Christmas Eve.

Sometimes an aspiring supermodel like yourself doesn't want to ruin her figure and abandon her career by filling up the house with kids only her husband is dying for. (Such an issue should have been discussed *before* the wedding, but you were too busy finalizing the divorce from your last marriage.) That said, if you don't want your husband to find out that you're still on the Pill, don't let him find the Pills.

On the other hand, your husband's resistance to having kids counts only as a minor obstacle on the road to conception. A bold woman like you with your equally bold maternal instincts can simply break into the fertility clinic where your husband sold sperm during his less noble years. Just don't expect him to jump for joy when you spring your little surprise on him during a romantic holiday. The act of impregnating you was not the part he'd been resisting.

Some couples have conceived children through in vitro fertilization. If you and your husband choose this option, keep a watchful eye on the fertilized eggs. Sit on them like a penguin if you have to. You certainly don't want your eggs winding up implanted in that crazy woman who's obsessed with your husband. (Don't think that it can't happen; she's crazy, but very persuasive with lab technicians.)

Other couples who have been trying to conceive a child without success have considered hiring a surrogate mother. For you, this offers some attractive pluses: a beautiful baby without nine months of morning sickness and eighteen hours of labor. There are downsides, though. For the next nine months, you will be ceding control of your home to this woman, who will be hormonal and demanding—more demanding than you, if you can believe that possible. You probably won't enjoy all the attention your husband will be paying to the mother of his child, but you might as well find a surrogate, where you have some say in the final choice, before you husband gets drunk and impregnates the maid.

Adoption offers another option, but one with a seri-

> Although obstetricians rarely recommend infidelity as a treatment for infertility, a one-night stand with an unsuitable partner (like your husband's black-sheep brother) will significantly increase your odds of conception.

ous drawback: The unwed mother, so grateful to you for giving her baby a home . . . a few months down the line, she's going to want her baby back, and she'll use the money you paid her to hire a cut-throat lawyer, who can make an excellent case on her behalf. When this happens, best to hand over the baby and wait until the girl discovers that she can't handle motherhood any better than she could her relationship with the baby's father.

(*Note: For the woman giving up her child, just know that*

no matter where you give a baby up, no matter where you move to afterward, that child will show up on your doorstep one day. They're like homing pigeons that way.)

Once your doctor confirms that you're pregnant, schedule a paternity test. If there are only two men who could be the father—and there really should be two, no more, no less—you don't need to bother both men for a blood sample. If it wasn't one fling, it was the other.

If the married man with whom you've been having an affair gets the results of the paternity test before you and bolts out of town with them, you don't need to bother with a retest; you can pretty safely bet that he just found out he's the father-to-be.

While pharmacies sell home pregnancy tests, the drug companies have yet to mass market home paternity tests. But you can do your own. Sit down and write the name of the two potential fathers on top of a piece of plain white paper. Calculate which man's life would be most complicated by this child or which man being the father would most complicate your life. Statistically, that man's name will match the results of the hospital's DNA test.

dangers for pregnant women to avoid

Medical experts advise pregnant women to avoid smoking, drinking, and excess stress. Good luck on that last one while you're trying to lead a soapier life. If you are half the vixen you imagine yourself to be, you're already sweating out the results of the inevitable paternity test. There are, however, nine months worth of dangers you can steer clear of if you want to give birth to your rich husband's sole heir.

staircases

Especially the long, winding variety rich people like your disapproving in-laws tend to favor in the foyer. Unless you plan on spending your entire pregnancy on ground level, stairs are a necessary evil, so hold the banister really tight and take a few extra precautions:

- Always check for steps that might have been loosened. If possible, send an envoy down ahead of you.
- Always look behind you before taking that first step. You never can tell which of your husband's crazy exes or even crazier relatives is sneaking up to give you a little shove.
- Most important, never be drawn into an argument at the top of a staircase. Pause, move down to the bottom, and resume fighting.

ladders

Aside from being rescued from a fire, there really is no reason for you to be on a ladder. Hanging drapes? Changing a lightbulb? Trimming the Christmas tree? If

"If you do happen to lose your footing and find yourself dangling over the edge, better to call out for the father of your baby rather than your husband, since your ex-lover's probably a little stronger . . ."

your husband can't afford to hire servants to do these things for you, then you might as well have just married the father of your child.

cliffs

You might survive falling off one—villains have a tendency to—but the baby might not fare so well. If you do happen to lose your footing and find yourself dangling over the edge, better to call out for the father of your baby rather than your husband, since your ex-lover's probably a little stronger, a little more capable of pulling you up to safety. (Isn't that why you got involved with him in the first place?) The heroic rescue will also provide the two of you with a legitimate excuse to steal a kiss that could lead to something more.

horses

Pregnant women no more belong in a stable than horses belong in the delivery room. Your oversensitivity to strong odors should keep you a great distance away. Even the best-groomed horse still smells like horse. And even the tamest will get spooked. He will spot a rattlesnake on the trail, or some vicious rival of yours will fire off a shotgun in the distance. If you're lucky, you'll get thrown to the ground; if not, you'll get dragged miles through the brush with your boot caught in the stirrup. If you need exercise, buy a bike . . . a stationary bike.

bank robberies

When it comes to hostage selection, you top every wish list: a two-for-one deal whose presence alone guarantees that the police won't be breaking out the tear gas. If the situation triggers an early labor, and it probably will, very few bank robbers are equipped to deliver a baby.

angry drivers

You cannot control the number of drunk and angry drivers on the road when you're coming home from a party late at night. But you can avoid getting into the car with one—especially if you're the one he's mad at. To minimize the possibility of your husband driving the two of you—make that the three of you—into a tree, you might want to wait until he's parked the car before you broach the subject of paternity tests.

elevators

Not a substantial risk until the tail end of your pregnancy. The moment the elevator gets stuck between floors, you will undoubtedly go into labor. If you absolutely must ride an elevator during your final trimester, do so only in hospitals, where you can increase the odds that one of the passengers stuck with you will be a doctor or nurse.

remote cabins

Even worse than elevators, where you would at least be inside a building with people who have a chance of knowing that you're trapped and going into labor. You may think that you need a few days at the family cabin to get away from all the stress, but you're only asking for trouble heading off into the woods by yourself. At the very least, check the weather reports for threats of torrential rain, blizzards, and flash flooding before you decide how much and how far you need to get away.

they grow up so fast (tips on child rearing)

The sooner you have your first daughter, the younger you will be when that girl begins dating. This will significantly increase your chances of eventually seducing the girl's boyfriend and/or fiancé. Don't be so moral about it. It's not like she won't be chasing after your husband once she's old enough.

Think about childbirth as a Yankee swap. You are rarely stuck with the baby that was just delivered. Maybe your father-in-law wanted his first grandchild to be a boy; old-money millionaires can be finicky like that. While the nurse in the maternity ward is off stealing drugs for her boyfriend, slip in and switch your pink bundle of joy with the boy from the crib beside her. Until the kid needs a blood transfusion, no one will be the wiser.

Be absolutely, 100 percent positive about your new son's paternity before you name him after your husband.

"While the nurse in the maternity ward is off stealing drugs for her boyfriend, slip in and switch your pink bundle of joy with the boy from the crib beside her. Until the kid needs a blood transfusion, no one will be the wiser."

The role of godparent is much too great a responsibility to entrust to anyone but the baby's biological father.

When your child is suffering from a high fever, cool her down with cold compresses and call your ex-husband to come sit by the bedside with you. He can hold your hand while you sit there holding your child's. When the fever finally breaks, you and your ex can share the sort of kiss that makes you wonder whether or not you should be getting back together.

Television is no substitute for parental attention and guidance. Make sure you find a boarding school that shares that philosophy.

Speaking of boarding schools, you can't ship your kids off to Europe when they're ten, then turn around and complain the next summer when they come home ready for college that you've missed out on their childhood.

YOU KNOW THIS IS ONE OF THOSE SOAP FIRST MEETINGS THAT LEAD TO A SUPERCOUPLE ROMANCE IF . . .

- ✓ You slap him across the face before hellos are even exchanged.
- ✓ He disappears after your dance without telling you his name.
- ✓ He pushes you out of the way of a speeding car.
- ✓ His motorcycle spooks the horse you are riding.
- ✓ You've walked in on him wearing nothing more than a towel.

faking an affair

When you are trying to break up a happy couple, you don't necessarily need to sleep with the husband. If you can seduce him at a weak moment, then by all means go for it. Usually, though, you need to separate him from the woman he loves before he becomes vulnerable to your charms. To expedite this break (which you can convince yourself would have occurred anyway in time), you only need to make it look as though the two of you have slept together. Toward this goal, several gambits have proven effective over the years . . .

the wine spill

Red wine works best for the following, the deeper the red the better—a nice merlot, for instance.

You invite the husband from across the hall in for a neighborly glass of wine. Since you'd like his wife to join the two of you when she gets home, you leave the apartment door more than a little ajar. During the course of the conversation, you "accidentally" spill your wine on

"

The man of your dreams is heading out of town on business. Alone. Wherever he's headed (hopefully a four-star hotel somewhere warm), find yourself a reason to be there, as well. Not just on the same island or in the same hotel, but in the suite directly across the hall from his.

"

his shirt, forcing him to remove it. If he resists, you insist that he needs to run it under cold water immediately; you would feel horrible if you had ruined such an obviously expensive shirt. Since you have undoubtedly set your sights on a soap hunk, he more than likely will not be wearing a T-shirt underneath. At that precise moment, the wife will be pushing the door open, only to see her husband standing there shirtless. While she may not think that anything happened this time, she will be left wondering how far things might have gone had she not come home when she did.

Plan B: If you can't spill the drink on him "accidentally," you *can* spill it on your own dress. As a gentleman, he will be obligated to help you unzip—which makes an even more questionable scenario for the wife to walk in on.

the pub crawl / bed crawl

When pulled off correctly, it creates the most damaging of tableaux.

Trail your target from bar to bar when he goes on one of his occasional benders, the sort that follows a really bad fight with his wife (the kind you and he will never have).

Buy him a few rounds while he bends your ear about his various marital woes. Once he has reached the point of intoxication, insist upon driving him home or, better yet, to some nearby motel to sleep it off. He really doesn't want his wife seeing him in this condition, does he?

As soon as he has passed out and you have finished undressing him (removing more than just his boots), you have a choice of two game plans:

1. You could slip into bed with him and let him wake up convinced that the two of you actually slept together. Why wouldn't he think that if he wakes up naked beside you in bed? His last memory of the night before was you taking his clothes off. That kind of guilt will eat away at him until he confesses all to his wife and she tosses him out.

2. For faster results, make sure the wife knows where she can find her husband. As a good friend to them both, why wouldn't you call the poor woman to let her know that her husband will not be coming home? Before you take off your clothes and slip into bed, leave the door slightly

ajar. The look on the wife's face when she walks in should tell you whether or not your ruse has worked. If she goes running from the room with a hand cupped over her mouth, consider your job well done.

As with the wine spill, your two biggest allies here are an open door and a well-timed arrival. If you hold up your end, fate usually plays its part with the timing.

the bedtime story

The Prince Charming you're trying to snag is a gentleman, is he not? If you get stranded at his home because of car trouble, he would not throw you out into the middle of a rainstorm just because his wife is out of town for the night. In chivalric manner, he will undoubtedly offer you the bed while he camps out on the couch. He probably won't even wake you up when he leaves for work in the morning. When his wife, tired from traveling all night, comes home, any reason you give for being in her bed, wearing her nightgown, will sound like a fairy tale—especially after you mutter her husband's name with a touch of lascivious affection while "waking up."

the surprise shower

You do not need to be caught in bed to raise a wife's suspicions. You can slip into the house just before the wife is due home from her trip and head straight for the upstairs bathroom, the one adjacent to the master bedroom. Stand in the shower until you hear someone rattling around, at which point you emerge clad only in a towel, calling the husband's name. When the wife asks what you were doing in her bathroom, gasp for breath and utter a few apologies before grabbing your clothes and running out the door.

the accidental tourism

The man of your dreams is heading out of town on business. Alone. Wherever he's headed (hopefully a four-star hotel somewhere warm), find yourself a reason to be there as well. Not just on the same island or in the same hotel, but in the suite directly across the hall from his. He'll be surprised—pleasantly, you hope—to see you coming out of your room in a swimsuit. Since you're both traveling alone, he'll invite you out to dinner. His wife won't be nearly so delighted by the coincidence, and may even question if it is one—especially after she calls his room and you answer.

the sour grapevine

You know all the pressure points for the gossip chain that runs through your town. If you've been living the life you should be, you've been the subject of talk since the day you wrecked your first home. You know how little to say to which person so that the story grows and grows and grows. Mention in passing to one local busybody that the man you're after sent you the most beautiful bouquet of flowers. The story that gets back to his wife will sound as though you and her husband have been fooling around for months.

the very very hotmail.com

That trip you took with her husband coupled with the local gossip will stir up the wife's suspicions, but you need to give her tangible proof of the affair. Tangible proof of an affair which has not yet begun? Impossible, you say? Not so, thanks to the Internet, the greatest weapon for marital sabotage since the camcorder.

Send yourself a romantic e-mail from his account, alluding in none too subtle terms to an evening of passion. His password should be relatively simple to figure out. Try his wife's birthday or his pet name for her. (You should remember these things because all the husband talked about during dinner that night in the islands was his wife.) When she checks his e-mail—which she will if you've planted your suspicions effectively—why wouldn't she believe it? It came from his own account.

the truth shall set him free

When the wife ultimately confronts you, deny all her accusations. For most people, this would be easy because it's true, but you have a rather tempestuous relationship with the truth. Here's where your reputation as a liar pays off big-time. Your repeated denials of anything going on with her husband will only confirm the wife's worst fears.

determining acceptable and unacceptable infidelity

Your less-than-faithful bridegroom slips away on your wedding night to sneak off for one last fling with his ex-girlfriend (more precisely, the last fling before he returns from the honeymoon). Not only do you know nothing about this other woman, you don't realize that the divorce from your first husband was never legalized. In the eyes of the law, that makes you, the cheated-upon wife, the adulteress—and your loathsome cad of a husband just another injured party.

Adultery, as daytime teaches us, isn't always a simple case of being in the wrong bed with the wrong person. Sometimes (but not as often as the cheating party would like), extenuating circumstances do need to be taken into consideration. Below are a number of situations in which you will more than likely find yourself, as well as some pointers on which acts of infidelity should be forgiven and which are grounds for divorce.

1. Your husband has been drinking heavily. In his stupor, he mistakes another woman for you. He mistakes her for you all the way back to her place.

   As an excuse, this holds water about as well as your husband holds his liquor.

2. You're suffering from a really bad case of the flu. The combination of a high fever and an overdose of medication has left you hallucinating. When your brother-in-law stops by with orange juice and aspirin, you envision him as your husband. You come on to him, he doesn't stop you, and both your temperatures climb a little bit higher.

   On the surface, this might look similar to the example above it: a mind-altering substance leading to a case of mistaken identity. The main difference is that your husband in the first example was drinking of his own free will; you were on medication while sick.

The fact that your brother-in-law found your runny nose so darn irresistible makes you wonder what he was on.

3. Your boyfriend heads down to the pond for a moonlight swim on a hot summer night and spots you standing there. No one else is around, so he pulls you into a kiss, and you respond. Wordless, one thing leads to another. When "you" finally speak after making love, your boyfriend realizes that he has just slept with your twin sister.

   If a man knows a woman well enough to be intimate with her, he should be able to tell the difference between her and her twin sister.

4. Imagine yourself the twin, the good twin. While your bad-boy husband loves you desperately, he has always been attracted to your bad-girl sister. One night, you fix your hair like hers, dress up in her clothes, and meet him at the door with a drink in hand. (As the good twin, you never touch anything stronger than wine.) Your husband responds to the seduction and takes you up

"To keep himself from pressuring you into sex, he has found himself a waitress of easy virtue and slipped into a short-term affair, a little something to tide him over until the wedding night."

to bed. You're now wondering, did my husband just cheat on me with myself?

Maybe your husband believed he was sleeping with your sister. Maybe he was going along with what he perceived as you role-playing. If he's smart, he'll never cop to the former. Bottom line, your husband didn't sleep with your sister; he slept with you, his wife, and you should really consider wearing your hair like that a little more often.

5. The secret agent with whom you're in love has broken into the home of a local crime lord, who just happens to be smitten with you. If this crime lord catches your lover in his house, he will have him executed, no questions asked. The only way you can think to keep the crime lord from returning home is to stall him with a seduction.

Your heart was definitely in the right spot. And you were panicking with good reason: The man you love was in real and immediate danger. Just don't expect him to appreciate your sacrifice anytime soon. He's going to feel doubly betrayed as a man. Not only did you sleep with someone else, you didn't trust that he, a secret agent, could protect himself.

6. Your husband dies in a horrible explosion. Grief-stricken, you turn to another man. The only thing is, your husband wasn't exactly blown to Kingdom Come. He's alive and well, and none too happy to discover that his wife has found herself a new boyfriend.

   Timing will determine the level of cheating here. If your husband has been wandering around with amnesia for the past five years, he can't exactly blame you for moving on. On the other hand, if he has returned midway through the funeral service . . .

7. You are a virgin and intend to remain one until the wedding night. Not only is your fiancé not a virgin, the time you have been dating is the longest period he's gone without sex since freshman year of high school. But he admires your decision. Your purity is one of the things he loves most about you. To keep himself from pressuring you into sex, he has found himself a waitress of easy virtue and slipped into a short-term affair,

a little something to tide him over until the wedding night.

Oh, the nobility. What a prince you have found in this young man, a martyr willing to sleep with a woman he doesn't love just to keep from pressuring you, the woman he loves, into giving him the sex he so desperately needs. If you don't detect the sarcasm here, then you are just as naïve as your fiancé believes you to be. A couple of things for you to ponder: (1) This waitress your fiancé's using is going along with this self-centered arrangement because she's in love with him; and (2) She is undoubtedly pregnant.

8. Your husband comes home early from a business trip, completely jet-lagged. With the lights off, he slips into bed with you, whom he has not seen in almost two weeks. When you stir, the two of you make love, then fall asleep in each other's arms. In the morning, with light streaming through the windows, he discovers his arms wrapped not around you but around your best friend, who was minding the house and the kids while you had to leave town on a family emergency.

When you come home from caring for a sick mother, you should love hearing all about how indistinguishable you are from every other woman in the dark. Maybe if your husband had been away two years, rather than two weeks, you might be able to justify a mix-up like this.

9. You and a male friend have been caught in an avalanche. While lying there, trapped under all that snow, thinking that he was going to die, your friend confessed that he has always loved you and wished that he could make love to you once before he died. Believing that neither one of you would make it out alive, you granted him what you thought would be his final wish. Now that you survived, you feel guilty, but you're not sure that it was really cheating.

   Traditional wedding vows read, "till death do us part," not "till an hour before I think I'm going to die do us part." Also, won't your husband appreciate knowing that you wanted to spend your final moments on earth making love to another man?

the fine line between love and hate

Psychologists firmly believe that there is a fine line between love and hate. Screaming "I hate you," for example, lacks credibility if you're ripping someone's clothes off while you say it. Nowhere is this line finer than on daytime television, where the very same couple accusing each other of adultery in front of a judge will be making love in the courthouse elevator on their way out. A criminal mastermind might one day find himself wooing the very same woman who would not even be alive if any of his death traps had ever worked properly; sometimes, against her better judgment and her family's wishes, the woman will find her former nemesis rather charming. From couples like these, you can learn cues to differentiate between pure hatred and that often very adulterated mix of love and hate.

The occasional nasty comment about the town cad lets everyone know that you're none too fond of him or his reputation with the ladies. The frequent nasty comment will leave your friends and family wondering how much you like saying this man's name.

You storm into the office of the corporate raider who's targeting your cosmetics company. While you're vowing that you will see him dead before he ever owns one piece of your company, the only way he can think to shut you up is to pull you into a kiss. If you indulge in the kiss for more than three seconds before slapping him across the face, you're not too eager to see him dead.

That brilliant but arrogant neurosurgeon has been driving you insane from the moment he joined the medical staff at the hospital where you work. The way he dismisses your opinions as though you didn't graduate from medical school yourself? You can't stand being in the same room with him. But if you stop by his apartment after dinner to discuss hospital matters that could easily wait until the next morning . . . well, you obviously *can* stand being in the same room with him.

To listen to you, God's gift to women turns your

> “That sleazeball lawyer you’ve been pitted against case after case asks you out to dinner—as if you don’t see more than enough of him in court every day.”

stomach—so much so that you can’t turn down his dinner invitation with a simple “No thank you.” No, you have to tell him, “I wouldn’t go out to dinner with you if I were starving to death.” If you honestly felt that strongly, then why are you so jealous of the way he turned around and asked out the first young lady who stepped off the elevator?

Of course the murder suspect you’re building a case against would be on your mind. You not only hate him for the murder he’s accused of, but for thinking that he’s above the law because he’s rich and sophisticated. He’s no different from the lowlifes you arrest every day—

except that you haven't been dreaming about making love to any of them.

That sleazeball lawyer you've been pitted against case after case asks you out to dinner—as if you don't see more than enough of him in court every day. You don't take the invitation any more seriously than the endless innuendoes he drops in the courthouse hallways. To you, they are the mind games of a lesser attorney trying to rattle you, and you resent his cheap tricks. On more than one occasion, you've threatened to bring sexual harassment charges against him. Maybe you don't hate those comments or the dinner invitations as much as you claim to, if you go running into the ladies' room to check your hair and makeup the first time he greets you with a professional, "Good morning, counselor," and nothing else.

The ladies' man from the office, who knew you were coming by his place to pick up a file, opens his door clad only in a towel. You can't believe that this wasn't planned; you also can't believe that he honestly expected you to respond to such an obvious stunt. Insulted by his latest juvenile maneuver, you roll your eyes to the heavens, but not for too long. You would like one more look before he puts on his bathrobe.

why good girls love bad boys . . .

You might tell all your friends that you're looking for a nice guy, but the moment some bad boy whizzes by on a stolen motorcycle, you can't shake the thought of making love to him. You will learn how to stitch up bullet wounds and spin convincing alibis for the thug you love. You will help your con artist boyfriend pull his scams. A bad boy can even sweet talk you into getting past the fact that he shot your father.

While Dr. Phil has his own hypotheses about what compels a good girl like yourself to fall in love with these bad boys, you can flip the channel over to any soap and find equally valid theories . . .

He's not as bad as people think.

Yes, he took you hostage on his yacht to give himself the advantage during "business negotiations" with your father. To be fair, though, he kept you in a stateroom more luxurious than most hotels you've stayed in. Outside of your initial fear that the food was drugged, you had no complaints. All the meals deserved four stars. Whenever he came in to check on you, his concern was real. You could see it in his eyes. Despite his varied crimes, including the murders he may (or may not) have ordered, you can see a good man inside him, a good heart.

You think you can change him.

Everyone grew up loving the whole "Beauty and the Beast" fairy tale, the way pure love transformed the hideous monster into a prince. While you're not vain enough to call yourself a beauty, you do believe that your love, which is pure, can transform your bad boy into a hero. What a testament to your desirability that a mob boss would give up his territory for you, the underworld equivalent to a king abdicating his throne. Just don't bank too much on the happily ever after. Once you've tamed the bad out of your boy, you might not find him quite so appealing.

You want to change yourself.

What has being the good girl gotten you? You lost your virginity to some frat boy who was only trying to win a bet. And now that rival fashion designer, a bad girl if you ever met one, has not only stolen your husband but all your ideas for the fall line as well. If you spend enough time with this bad boy, maybe some of his less than noble traits—especially his tenacity for seeking revenge—could rub off, making you less of a target in the future.

He's protective of you.

The world is filled with really bad men, not bad boys you can fall in love with, but bad men who operate far outside the boundaries of the law and human decency. The police may arrest these baddies every third or fourth crime, but the charges never stick. When you get kidnapped by a bad man, you need a bad boy looking for you, someone who isn't worried about violating a henchman's civil rights.

This relationship will tick off your family.

Your status-conscious parents never liked any of the boys you brought home. Your first crush didn't come from the right sort of family. That musician you dated in college lacked ambition and prospects for the right sort of future. Bringing a mobster home to dinner will make your parents and grandfather regret buying and/or scaring off those other guys.

Things will never get boring with him.

If you listened to your mother, you would have married that up-and-comer at your father's law firm. While his job is interesting, you will never be part of it unless you wind up as opposing counsel. The bad boy, on the other hand, always brings his work home. If he's not hiding a briefcase full of cash under your bed, it's some microchip jam-packed with government secrets. Midway through his latest caper, you can count on an intruder breaking in during the middle of the night. Maybe it's one of the good guys, maybe not. Either way, your bad boy will be suiting you up with a black wig and whistling you out of town for two thrilling months of life on the run.

infatuation, true love, or obsession?

Sadly, you can't always tell the difference between true love and infatuation until it has run its course, which you can only hope it has done for your lover as well. You also do not want to be the one clinging onto a relationship long after the point where he's not only stopped caring, he's stopped answering your calls.

One little warning bell to listen to . . . Unrequited love crossed the line into obsession the minute you started building that cage in your basement. But as long as you're intent on holding your "soul mate" captive until he realizes that you're the one he truly loves—which will be never—the merciful thing would be to install plumbing facilities.

Some more warning bells on differentiating between infatuation, love, and obsession . . .

It might only be infatuation if . . .

. . . you think he looks cool riding around on his motorcycle with his long hair blowing in the wind.

You know it's true love when . . .

. . . you insist that he start wearing a helmet.

It's crossed the line into obsession once . . .

. . . you cut the brake lines so you can nurse him back to health after he crashes.

It might only be infatuation if . . .

. . . you're writing his name with little hearts around it on the covers of all your notebooks.

You know it's true love when . . .

. . . you're signing his name and yours on Christmas cards.

It's crossed the line into obsession once . . .

. . . you've forged his name onto a marriage license.

It might only be infatuation if . . .

. . . those pictures of you kissing in the photo booth? Half the strip is taped inside his locker, the other half inside yours.

You know it's true love when . . .

. . . you're videotaping him teach the kids how to ride a bike.

It's crossed the line into obsession once . . .

. . . you've pasted your own face over his wife's throughout their wedding album.

It might only be infatuation when . . .

. . . you come up with cute nicknames for each other.

You know it's true love when . . .

. . . after five years of marriage, you still enjoy referring to each other as "Mr." and "Mrs."

It's crossed the line into obsession once . . .

. . . you will only answer when addressed by his wife's name.

It might only be infatuation if . . .

. . . your disapproving parents can't keep him away.

You know it's true love when . . .

. . . armed guards at every door can't keep him away.

It's crossed the line into obsession once . . .

. . . a restraining order won't keep him away.

It might only be infatuation if . . .

. . . you're just kids.

You know it's true love when . . .

. . . you want to have his kids.

It's crossed the line into obsession once . . .

. . . you have his kids—and he will never see them again unless he does exactly what you say.

YOU KNOW YOU'RE ONE OF THE "GOOD" SOAP MOBSTERS IF . . .

✓ The only people you ever kill are the bad mobsters, meaning the ones who sell drugs to children and terrorize women.

✓ You look really handsome in a tuxedo.

✓ You show up at all of the hospital fund-raisers, pledging million-dollar donations.

✓ You have fathered children with upstanding members of the community—like the district attorney.

✓ No one, not even your district attorney ex, has been able to convict you of any crimes—maybe because no one can tell exactly what crimes you do commit, aside from occasionally rubbing out these other mobsters.

what to expect from a life on the force

If you join the police force, don't go in with painfully unrealistic expectations of solving crimes and locking up the bad guys. The majority of people you arrest will be innocent, and the murders will usually be solved by your teenaged sister and her boyfriend.

You can also rule out any dreams of one day being named commissioner. That position is reserved for ex-spies (even traitors), reformed jewel thieves, former mercenaries, and the occasional record executive.

More realistic expectations for a police officer would be . . .

1. You will be arresting members of your own family.

   At the very least, you will be pulling them in for questioning on a regular basis. As you rise in the department, you will eventually be able to exercise a modicum of discretion. You may, for instance, be allowed to wait until after your sister has said her "I do" before you slap on the cuffs.

2a. At some point, you will be going undercover as a dirty cop.

   For the sake of the assignment, you'll need to break up with your boyfriend, but you won't be able to tell him why.

2b. During this time, your boyfriend, who is technically an ex even if he doesn't feel that way to you, will date the same criminal you've gone undercover to bring down.

   The more you warn him to stay away, the more he will dig in his heels; he may even marry the criminal just to spite you.

3. You will be shot.

4. You will be shot again.

   One of these two shots will leave you:

   a. blind

   b. comatose

   c. paralyzed from the waist down

   d. unable to have kids

   or

   e. addicted to pain pills

5. Your life will be saved at least once by the very same mobster you have been trying to arrest since your first day on the force.

   To thank him, you will look the other way the one and only time you'll ever have the chance to charge him with something that could stick.

6. Your best friend will be taken hostage.

   The fugitive doesn't even have to be gunning for you in particular. He'll just grab your best friend at random and use her as a body shield during his standoff with the police, meaning you. Of course, you're going to put down your gun when he points the one he's hold-

"You can also rule out any dreams of one day being named commissioner. That position is reserved for ex-spies (even traitors), reformed jewel thieves, former mercenaries, and the occasional record executive."

ing at your friend's "pretty little head." Just pray that your partner, who's hiding behind some crates, has been spending his free nights at the firing range.

7. You will sleep with a suspect.

   The fact that he turns out to be innocent may save your job, but it won't win you any points with your boyfriend.

8. You will be told to turn in your gun and badge at least once.

   With the number of rules you've broken and the times you've disobeyed a direct order to wait for backup, you're lucky you haven't been suspended before now.

9. You will continue to work on at least one murder investigation after being taken off the case.

   Ironically, this will be the one case you actually solve. You'll figure out whodunit, but since you did so on your own time without any authority, you won't break the department's losing streak.

10. You will ultimately quit the force over procedural demands and open your own private investigation agency.

expanding your miranda rights

Anyone who has grown up watching prime-time cop shows can recite the Miranda Rights by heart ("You have the right to remain silent; anything you say can and will be used against you; you have the right to a lawyer," yada yada yada.) But for soap audiences, who watch their favorites get arrested several times a year, these rights are painfully limited and should be expanded.

You not only have a right to be silent, you have a right to sulk all day long in your prison cell, refusing to acknowledge any of the visitors who come to see you.

You have the right to confess to murder if you legitimately believe that the woman you love may have committed the crime.

You have the right to frame your ex-wife's fiancé for the murder if you believe it is the only way she'll finally see that he is completely wrong for her.

You have the right, when arriving upon a murder scene, to pick up the gun lying next to the dead body, thus leaving a clear set of your prints on the weapon.

"You have a right to propose marriage to the one woman whose testimony could prove most damaging to your case. If you are considered too great a flight risk to even be allowed to go to church, the wedding ceremony may be performed in interrogation room B."

You have the right to remind the arresting officers what a powerful man you are in this state and that your good friend, the governor, with whom you play poker every Wednesday night, can break them down to meter maids by morning.

You have a right to propose marriage to the one woman whose testimony could prove most damaging to your case. If you are considered too great a flight risk to even be allowed to go to church, the wedding ceremony may be performed in interrogation room B.

You have a right to jump bail if that time will be used for your personal investigation into the murder. Penalties for crossing state lines will be waived if your investigation entails you joining a traveling circus.

You have the right to representation by a lawyer who does not still harbor a secret lifelong grudge against your family.

If you cannot afford a lawyer, the court will appoint the district attorney's feisty ex-wife, who is more than willing to take on your case pro bono just for the opportunity to make a fool of her former husband in public.

while on trial for murder

At some point in your life, you are going to be arrested for murder. Everyone you have ever publicly threatened to kill has wound up shot, stabbed, poisoned, or tossed off the balcony of their hotel room.

Don't be naïve enough to assume that being innocent will keep you from going to prison. The district attorney's office has an unusually high success rate for convicting innocent men and women. A really handsome district attorney can convict you of murder when no one was even killed.

If you come from one of those upstanding families that doesn't keep a lawyer on retainer—or if you won't accept your rich mother's help because of her sleeping with your ex—you need to find yourself a good attorney, one who knows his way around the court system. Before hiring him to represent you, there are some questions you need to ask:

a. Have you ever worked a little less zealously to defend a client because you wanted to put the moves on his girlfriend while he's in prison?

b. Have you ever defended a client for a murder you yourself committed?

c. Have you ever been temporarily disbarred for trying to persuade a jury to convict your client?

d. Have you ever been called by the prosecution to testify against your own client?

If your lawyer denies all of these questions, assume that he's lying. If he's done so convincingly, sign him on because your trial has been moved up.

While you have hired a lawyer to speak on your behalf, no one expects you to sit there quietly for the entire duration of the trial. You know the witnesses better than your lawyer. You know when one of them is lying through her teeth just to make sure you fry. If your lawyer won't object, then stand up for yourself. Start shouting at the witness, "That's a lie, and you know it!" Then turn to the jury and fill them in: "She's lying. You can't believe a word she's saying."

The judge won't take too kindly to this outburst, and even less so the second time you do it. But you'd be robbing yourself of the full courtroom experience if you were not threatened with contempt at least once.

When your brother is called to testify against you, your mother can interrupt from where she's sitting. "How," she can ask him, ". . . how can you say these things against your own sister?" Again, the judge won't be pleased; he may even threaten to clear the courtroom, but they never make good on threats like that.

When your lawyer is bearing down on your ex-husband, pressuring him to confess to an affair with the deceased that would make him look like a suspect, order your lawyer to back off. Threaten to fire him if you have to. Your ex will always remember the way you defended him and regret telling the police that he thinks you committed the murder. (Note: If your lawyer thinks he can badger your ex into admitting that he still loves you, that you can allow. It'll make for a bright spot in this whole dreary experience.)

A key witness to your defense needs to be hiding out in a foreign country. He or she needs to be shuttled straight to the courtroom from the airport and called to the stand at the very last second. Of course, this name will not have been pre-announced on the witness list. The district attorney will call this maneuver "highly irregular," like it doesn't happen during every single murder trial in your town.

Should you need to be out of town, even out of the country for a day or two during your trial, it is perfectly acceptable for an identical twin to sit in for you at the defense table.

Constitutionally, you do not have to testify against yourself. In fact, your lawyer would highly recommend that you steer clear of the witness box. Just bear in mind one thing. The court papers read: "The State v. Your Name," not your attorney's. That makes this *your* show. If you want a solo performance, you walk right up, swear yourself in, and commit a little perjury.

The prosecution, it should be noted, is expecting you to perjure yourself. Your testimony wouldn't be any fun for him if you didn't give him a lie he could expose with Exhibit V, the surveillance tape from the convenience store.

Despite your outbursts and the blatant lies you told, the jury may still find you not guilty. (Maybe your rich daddy was able to buy off a juror or two.) Should you be declared not guilty, you still need to get out of the courtroom. Don't be surprised if the grief-stricken girlfriend of the deceased grabs the bailiff's gun and dishes out her own justice. When you survive the gunshot, compassion demands that you not press charges against her.

Unless the amateur sleuths around town have uncovered the real killer, you will more than likely be found guilty of murder in the first degree. When you are, you really want the death penalty. You also want your execution scheduled for no more than two months down the road. The tight deadline will light a fire under your defense attorney, your ex-husband, and the one cop who now believes that you're innocent. If you were given a life sentence, they wouldn't feel anywhere near the same urgency to find the real killer.

As the bailiffs are dragging you from the courtroom, handcuffed, keep shouting, "I'm innocent. I didn't do it. I'm innocent. Innocent!"

when summoned to testify at a murder trial

No one likes getting subpoenaed to testify in a trial, much less a murder trial. It feels like a lot of bother for someone else's big day. But don't fret because you are not the star in this particular courtroom. One day, you will most definitely find yourself on trial for murder.

To be honest, testifying in a murder trial is really not that big an imposition. You cannot even call it a waste of your time. You were going to the courtroom anyway to show support for the defendant or maybe for the sister of the victim . . . Actually, you were going for a front row seat to the best show in town, the current place to see and be seen. Being called to testify not only guarantees you admission into the courtroom, which may be closed to the general public, it will also guarantee that you will be seen—albeit in a minor (but far from unimportant) role.

For the hour or so that you are sitting in the witness box, every ear in the courtroom (the jury, the district attorney, the judge, the defendant, the spectators) will be listening to your every syllable. All eyes will be focused upon you. The jury may glance over at the defendant to catch a reaction or two every once in a while, but you are the one to whom they are obligated to pay attention. Unlike the defendant, you get to sit facing the reporters and gossip seekers. They get to see more of you than the back of your head.

To maximize your time in the witness box, you do need to follow certain rules. We're not just talking about swearing to tell the truth, the whole truth, and so on. That rule should be obeyed only in so far as it enhances your overall courtroom experience. If you adhere to the following, your testimony will become the highlight of the entire trial.

Don't sit around waiting for the subpoena.

As soon as you realize that you're going to be called to testify, start hiding from the summons server. Make him work for that commission. You don't want to seem too easy to find. You don't want him or anyone else thinking that you have so little to do with your day that you can sit around a courtroom. Plus, the harder you are to locate, the more desirable you become. (You've undoubtedly come to appreciate the hard-to-get principle with more than a few suitors.) After a week or so hunting you down, the district attorney will be salivating at the thought of putting you in the witness box, confident that you must be hiding something pretty important.

Wait in the hallway.

Do not sit in the courtroom before you are called to the stand. You don't make half as powerful or dignified a first impression climbing over the legs of the trial gawkers who grabbed the aisle seats. Waiting in the hallway will allow you a grand entrance. Your name will announced: "For my next witness, I call to the stand . . . " Make the bailiffs hold not one but both doors open so that you can walk down the middle of the aisle.

There's no need to state your real name.

It doesn't matter that you've taken an oath to tell the truth; the name you've been living under since you arrived in town will suit the prosecutor's immediate needs just fine. Save revealing your true identity for a gathering that's all about you and you alone.

Be a hostile witness.

Develop a contentious relationship with the prosecutor from the very beginning. When he asks if you were sexually involved with the victim, tell him that it's none of his business. When he pushes, turn the question around onto him. Ask him, "Have you ever been in love?" He'll ask the judge to remind you that he's the one asking the questions. Smile and enjoy the fact that a man like this, who obviously prefers to talk about himself all day long, is being forced to ask you questions about yourself. In a courtroom, nothing tells the jury and spectators that you are special more than the judge allowing the district attorney to treat you as a hostile witness. The animosity between you and the DA will create much needed drama for all the poor jurors who have just feigned attentiveness during a two-hour cross-examination about gunpowder residue.

Avoid answering with a simple "Yes" or "No."

The district attorney and even the judge may admonish you to answer the questions posed to you with a simple "Yes" or "No." As if you'd allow anyone to write your dialogue. When the prosecutor asks if you were acquainted with the deceased, a simple "Yes" is painfully forgettable. The proper response to such an inquiry is: "Yes, I knew that monster, and he deserved what he got."

Point with enthusiasm.

Since you were an eyewitness to key events, you will be asked to identify the person you saw running out of the office on the night of the murder. The prosecutor will not only ask you to state whom you saw, he will instruct you to point to that person in the courtroom. This gives you a chance to throw your whole body into the testimony. Your index finger will shake with hesitation. You will wait until the prosecutor repeats himself, prodding, forcing you as if against your will. Reluctantly, you will not only point at the defendant, but stand up to do so with a full extension of your arm. You will then collapse back into your chair from the emotional exhaustion.

"As soon as you realize that you're going to be called to testify, start hiding from the summons server. Make him work for that commission. You don't want to seem too easy to find."

Make at least one inflammatory observation.

Since the prosecutor has gone to the trouble of bringing you into a courtroom, you owe him a little something. When he asks you to describe the defendant's appearance when you spotted her fleeing the murder scene, he has rolled out the red carpet for elaboration. Look at the jury and say, "She looked as though she had just killed somebody."

Make a confession of your own.

During the cross-examination, you need to snap under the pressure. Break down in tears and confess that you were once a prostitute, that you let strange men have their way with you for money. Then, through your tears, you must look up at the defense attorney, stare him square in the eye, and ask, "Is that what you wanted me to say? Is that what you wanted to hear?"

Force a break.

The confession about your sordid past has obviously taken its toll on you. So you enjoy a good long cry. Neither the district attorney nor the defense counsel will risk their case by bullying you into stopping.

Even the judge knows he would come across like an absolute ogre if he turned down your request for a recess. Try to plan this request close to the end of the day so that the judge will adjourn the trial until the following day. People will leave the courtroom talking about you and wondering all night what you will be revealing next.

Drop a few more bombshells.

You cannot disappoint your public. They deserve to hear everything you've been holding back till you had a big enough audience. If the defendant was having an affair behind her husband's back, now's the time to let that cat out of the bag. Maybe it wasn't the defendant having the affair. Maybe it was someone else who is sitting in the courtroom as an observer. Never worry how relevant your information is to the case. That's the jury's job, to sift through all the facts and decide. When you are subsequently confronted by the people whose secrets you've exposed, fall back on the excuse, "I was under oath. I had to tell the truth."

career options for ex-hookers

From the teenaged street hustler to the high-class call girl, the hooker with a heart of gold remains a soap staple. At least the ones who choose to reform do. Once you decide to get off the street, you need to figure out how to make a living that will keep you in the style to which you've become accustomed, a style that includes collecting artwork and paying tuition for secret children at high-priced boarding schools.

While not exactly the sort of thing you can include on your résumé, prostitution does prepare you quite well for a variety of career choices, although very few that pay anything close to what you were pulling in tax-free.

nurse

It certainly helps if you don't freak out around naked bodies of the opposite sex. And it's not like you've never dressed up in a nurse's uniform for one of your clients.

hairdresser

Let's face it, no one has more practice fixing hair and makeup several times a day (or night, as the case may be).

cosmetics executive

Again, who knows more than you about the extreme challenges makeup can face?

marriage counselor

You've listened for years to men complaining about their wives. You may actually find it refreshing to hear the women's side of the story. (Just remember, you're not supposed to lie down next to them on the couch.)

“From the teenaged street hustler to the high-class call girl, the hooker with a heart of gold remains a soap staple. At least the ones who choose to reform do.”

police officer

You'll be walking the same cruddy streets in the same seedy sections of town you used to prowl in the midnight hours. Now you will be able to do so with a gun.

restaurant chanteuse

In your life, you've already done a lot worse than sing for your supper.

waitress

It's all about service with a smile.

hotelier

As a madam, you ran a twenty-five-room bordello. The only real difference between that and a five-star hotel are the amenities.

nun

Some prostitutes seek redemption for their sinful pasts by throwing themselves into a lifetime of complete commitment to God. Since you've already more than met your sex quota for this lifetime, the whole celibacy vow should not present a major obstacle.

(Note: Sadly for the average pimp, unless he bears a remarkable resemblance to his doctor brother, whose life and career he can take over, job prospects post-pimping are extremely narrow, usually limited to blackmailer and con artist.)

the best targets for blackmail

If the modeling assignments have stopped coming in and you've run out of old engagement rings to hock, you may be considering a new career in blackmail. It's not completely removed from the glamorous world of news reporting, but instead of broadcasting information you've uncovered, you'll be paid for keeping it to yourself.

As with any new business venture, you need to find your market. For you, that will be not only people with secrets they don't want coming back to haunt them, but people who can afford your fees. Let's face it, unless that maid knows the combination to her millionaire boss's wall safe, she can't pay you much to keep quiet about some babies she switched thirty years ago.

Some potentially lucrative targets to consider . . .

reformed prostitutes

So many move on to respectable lives: high-profile jobs and wealthy husbands—husbands who might not be too happy to find out that they are very, very far from the first man to see their wife naked. Even if they already know and love their wife in spite of the past, they don't want all their business associates knowing.

"If the modeling assignments have stopped coming in and you've run out of old engagement rings to hock, you may be considering a new career in blackmail."

unrepentant gigolos

An "old friend" of yours seems to have quite the knack for romancing lonely widows out of their fortunes. Once you find out where he's running his latest scam, you invest your last few dollars in a bus ticket. Then, he either cuts you in for a piece of the action or you spill all you know to his latest pigeon. As a down payment and show of good faith, he can set you up with a nice room in the widow's mansion.

gay politicians

There is absolutely nothing wrong with a politician being gay. Unless he's killing people to keep his secret from his wife and constituents—which gives you even more to blackmail him about.

cheatin' spouses

Just grab your camcorder and wander around the docks late at night or check out the hospital stairwells. Sooner or later, you'll stumble upon at least one couple who is married, but not to each other.

your ex-lovers—specifically your married ex-lovers

The romantic in you has kept every love letter from that married man you were seeing last year. The pragmatist in you realizes that this guy would probably pay dearly to get those letters back, along with all those photos of the two of you together. You don't even need to call it blackmail. You can think of it as him continuing to give you little gifts the way he was thrilled to do back when he was cheating on his wife. Just remember the economics of supply and demand: This box of love letters triples, maybe even quadruples in value should your ex-lover ever head into divorce court, where a judge will be determining alimony.

your future mother-in-law

This woman would rather eat her own pearls than welcome a gold-digging schemer like you into the family. If she doesn't come to you first with a reasonable bribe to walk away from her son, you need to initiate the conversation. Be careful to keep your language vague and wax poetic about your love for the woman's son, just in case she's taping you. You don't want to wind up the blackmail*ee*.

non-biological fathers

If he can pay off lab technicians to falsify paternity results, he obviously has deep pockets. And if he's willing to assume the financial burden for a child that isn't his own, there's no reason why he can't also be putting your kids through college.

alcoholic doctors

They have all botched one or two surgeries back when they were boozing it up. Since they wouldn't still be practicing medicine if it wasn't for you keeping their little secret, that should entitle you to a percentage of their six-figure salaries—retroactively, of course. When they tell you that you're scum, just remind them how appreciative they were of your help back when you were covering up their mistakes.

heart patients

It really isn't that surprising what heart patients will agree to do or sign when you're holding their bottle of pills.

YOU KNOW YOU'RE SEEING A SOAP DOCTOR IF . . .

- ✓ That miracle drug he claims will save your life is not just experimental, it's something he whipped up that morning in his secret lab.
- ✓ He has medical files on your mother dating all the way back to her childhood—and she's not even his patient!
- ✓ You wouldn't be in need of his surgical skills if he hadn't been trying to kill you.
- ✓ He won't write you a prescription for the painkillers you've become addicted to, but he will drop off a bottle at your house this evening.
- ✓ He has to mop the hospital floors in between office visits as part of his community service agreement with the court.

what they don't teach you in medical school

Medical school may very well be the single biggest scam pulled on aspiring doctors. The truth of the matter is this: You don't need to go to med school to be a doctor. A college diploma would be nice, but even that isn't a prerequisite for the wealthy and the well connected. No, hospitals are run just like every other family business. Anyone with ambition, a modicum of brains, and a grandparent on the board of directors can work their way up. Of course, medical schools will never admit this. They would be putting themselves out of business.

Naturally, you won't become a doctor your very first day on the job. You'll start off slow, as an aide or a physical therapist, but after a few months of walking around, wearing the white lab jacket, people will start calling you "Doctor." Not too long after that, other doctors will be pulling you aside for consults and inviting you to observe the open heart surgery they're doing that afternoon. Pay close attention because pretty soon you'll be the one delivering babies and transplanting kidneys.

Pay really close attention to what's happening around you, and you will discover all of the medical profession's dirtiest little secrets . . .

- Like med schools, hospitals themselves are just another money-making scheme.

- Patients also don't need sterile operating rooms. Soap mothers have been proving this for decades, giving birth every place imaginable outside of a delivery room. You'll see the operating room for the needless luxury it is after you've removed a bullet from some mobster's chest using nothing more than a pair of tweezers and a bottle of vodka for anesthetic—all in the comfort of his own hideout. (If you have gone the med school route, a grateful mobster can put a healthy dent in those hefty student loans.)

- Cardiologist . . . neurosurgeon . . . fertility specialist . . . Medical specialties give you impressive titles but little else. At the end of the day, you're all doctors, and you're all interchangeable. In a pinch, even a psychiatrist can perform complicated heart surgery.

"With the right medication, a warm fire, and the occasional visit from a nurse, patients can recover from the flu or pneumonia just as effectively in an isolated cabin as they can in some overpriced hospital ward."

- Hospitals only need two or three doctors on hand at any given time. Even one will do, if she's well respected.

- If you want to be considered the top specialist in any field, you cannot live in the United States. You need to move to Switzerland. Wealthy patients never trust their American doctors with anything more involved than a simple appendectomy. They always insist upon flying in an expert from some private overseas clinic. This might very well be related to them drinking only imported champagne and wearing only French designers.

- Medical schools offer courses in bedside manner under the pretense that they will make you a better doctor. This sort of sensitivity training is to be avoided like the plague, even if the upperclassmen promise that it's an easy A. Hand-holding and lollipops may help pediatricians build their practice, but a kind smile will flatline all your surgical aspirations. A young doctor, especially a beautiful young surgeon, will never be acknowledged as brilliant unless she is cold as ice.

- That whole taboo about patient confidentiality can be circumvented by admitting, "I really shouldn't be telling you this" before revealing a patient's entire medical history to any interested third party.

- Lobotomies and other such illegal operations can be performed, but only after midnight and only in the abandoned sections of the hospital.

- You are going to be tempted to let the occasional patient die under your knife. It's just not rewarding saving the life of some psycho who has tried to murder half the people you work with. While the Hippocratic oath forbids you to refuse treatment or intentionally nick one of his important arteries, "proper care" does allow you a certain amount of leeway. You'll want to keep the patient sedated; someone with a history of violence like his, you might want to keep restrained as well. If this leaves him a tad vulnerable to any of his would-be victims who stop by, that does not reflect negatively on the brilliant operation you performed.

stocking the medicine cabinet

You may not be able to find all the following at your local CVS, but you know plenty of people who work at the hospital and a few doctors of questionable ethics. Between the two, you can stock up on pretty much everything you need.

knockout drops and chloroform

Sometimes when you need a certain someone unconscious to ransack his apartment or to have him spirited away to your dungeon, you can enjoy the luxury of drugging his wine and sitting down with him until it takes effect. You always love that look in a victim's eyes when he realizes that he's been drugged. In cases like this, knockout drops will do the job very nicely. But you don't always have time for such cat-and-mouse games. You need someone out cold *now*. And you don't want them knowing it was you when they wake up. In that case, you need to sneak up behind them with a chloroform-soaked rag. One caveat: Should you go the chloroform route, don't use one of your monogrammed handkerchiefs.

an aphrodisiac

Don't take this as an insult. Yes, everyone knows that men have left their wives for you. Men have risked their lives, rushing into the Amazon to rescue you from the mercenaries who hijacked your plane. Unfortunately, even someone as sexy and desirable as yourself needs a little help now and again with men who are stubbornly faithful to their wives.

birth control pills

Not that you're taking them. You just need to leave the case on a shelf where it can't be missed. The guy you want to get you pregnant might not be so diligent about taking precautions of his own if he thinks you're on the

Pill. If he has seen the case, he can hardly accuse you of having trapped him into fatherhood.

a pregnancy test and mouthwash

Not all home pregnancy tests are alike, not when you need to fake a pregnancy. Buy the kit with the stick that turns blue if you're having a baby. You need to also pick up blue-colored mouthwash. (Almost every brand carries a blue version.) You probably see where this is headed . . .

(Note: An added bonus for someone who kisses as much as you, the mouthwash can also be used as mouthwash.)

an amnesia-inducing drug

You don't always need to have a romantic rival killed. In truth, you only need to wipe out the woman's memory of the last few years, the years she spent falling in love with the man you want. Unfortunately, this drug doesn't have a name, but you tell your doctor friend what you need it for, and he'll custom brew something special.

"Not all home pregnancy tests are alike, not when you need to fake a pregnancy. Buy the kit with the stick that turns blue if you're having a baby. You need to also pick up blue-colored mouthwash."

poison

Like picking out the bottle of wine you're going to be drugging, there are a mind-boggling number of poisons to choose from. Ideally, you'd like something colorless so that you can add it not only to red wine but white, as well. Or even a glass of water. You also want to be looking for a poison with no taste. Your victim is not going to finish his drink if it tastes funny. You probably also want a slow-acting poison, something that will kick in later on, preferably when he's not sitting on your couch—unless you don't mind disposing of yet another dead body. (One note of caution: Never place both his poisoned glass of wine and your own on a lazy Susan.)

antitoxin

The enemy you're inviting over for wine probably knows how much you hate him. It's not like you've kept your feelings a big secret. Your invitation has undoubtedly raised a few red flags. If you're asking him over for the sole purpose of poisoning him, he may have accepted because he's coming over with the sole intention of doing the same to you.

sodium pentathol (truth serum)

You can go to the trouble of chaining your enemy up in the basement, denying him food and water till he tells you what you need to know—but you know what a consummate liar he is. It's much quicker and far more reliable to simply pump him full of truth serum before you begin the interrogation.

zombie powder

At some point, you're going to need to fake your own death. That's one of those inescapable givens that comes with being a soap heroine. A little sprinkle of zombie powder can paralyze you and leave your breathing so shallow it's undetectable. Just make sure that you have an extremely trustworthy accomplice who won't let you be embalmed, autopsied, or cremated.

spare toothbrush

Because you never know who will be spending the night . . . Who are we kidding? You know exactly who you will be seducing and on what night.

smelling salts

If you're leading the sort of life you should be, there will be a significant amount of fainting taking place in your living room.

Keep these drugs in your medicine cabinet until you use them—at which point, it's time to get rid of the evidence.

> "You probably also want a slow-acting poison, something that will kick in later on, preferably when he's not sitting on your couch—unless you don't mind disposing of yet another dead body."

when choosing your psychiatrist . . .

When choosing a psychiatrist, just bear in mind that a medical degree is no guarantee of sanity. The serial killer the police are hunting down might very well be the psychologist they've brought in to create the killer's profile. So try to find a shrink who's no crazier than you. You probably want someone who has never held you hostage while imagining himself to be his dead brother, or tried to blow up your apartment complex.

Anyone can hang a diploma on their wall and call themselves a psychiatrist. Of all the medical professions, it's still the easiest one to fake. You sit there, listen, and ask questions like, "How does that make you feel?" During your first session, take a moment to make sure that the name on that diploma matches the one on the office door. And that they're both spelled the same way.

Like all other medical professionals, psychiatrists are bound by the code of patient confidentiality. That means that they're not *supposed* to reveal anything you tell them. But it's only a code. It's not some magic spell that keeps them from speaking. It certainly didn't prevent your obstetrician from letting your chief-of-staff father find out you were pregnant.

Lots of psychiatrists like to record their sessions. They tell you that the tapes help with the treatment. Those tapes can also come back to haunt you whenever the psychiatrist is strapped for cash. Even if your psychiatrist himself is above blackmail, he isn't storing those tapes in Fort Knox. Any one of your enemies can break into the office and discover all the embarrassingly intimate details of your life. Don't just forbid the doctor to tape your sessions, have your techies do a complete sweep of the office.

Marriage counseling can steer many a couple through the rough patches, but not as effectively if it's being conducted by a therapist with the hots for your husband.

Sometimes when you witness a murder, your mind

just blanks it out. You try and you try, but you just can't seem to remember who it was you saw pull the trigger. Hypnosis sounds like the perfect solution, an instant fix for unlocking those memories. Before you start counting backward from a hundred, you might want to check with the police on how high up your psychiatrist is on the list of suspects. Honestly, you don't want to be semi-

"So try to find a shrink who's no crazier than you. You probably want someone who has never held you hostage while imagining himself to be his dead brother, or tried to blow up your apartment complex."

conscious and alone in a dark room with the killer whose freedom hinges on you never telling what you've seen.

If you are faking some sort of insanity to avoid an attempted murder charge, you don't want any experts flown in; you want a psychiatrist fresh out of medical school, bottom of his class.

It is really easy to fall in love with your psychiatrist. Here is an accomplished man who puts time aside to listen to your problems, an intelligent man who wants to talk about your feelings. Should such a man opt to ignore the whole ethical issue about dating patients and return your affection, you may feel like the luckiest woman in the world. Just bear in mind that you are more than likely not the first patient to fall in love with this particular shrink. In other words, your dream wedding has just made you the major obstacle standing between some obsessed lunatic and the man of her dreams.

It's never easy committing a loved one to a mental facility, even if it's for their own good. You will feel a little better about your decision if you find them a place where the criminally insane patients can't come and go as they please more easily than you can get in for a visit.

when considering plastic surgery . . .

Maybe a frustrated gambler threw acid in your face when your boxer boyfriend refused to take a dive. Maybe that tumble through the skylight in your penthouse has left you with a highly visible scar. Perhaps you're being paid a lot of money to be transformed into the spitting image of some mob boss's dead wife. Whatever your reason—and each one is equally valid—just make sure you put more effort into picking your plastic surgeon than you did your second husband.

If your plastic surgeon is a widower, feel him out to see how *devoted* he remains to his late wife. Keeping a photo of the woman on his desk is normal. Walls covered with pictures of her in a secret shrine should raise a few red flags.

Sometimes, you don't have much choice in picking a plastic surgeon. If your car explodes within dragging distance of the man's private clinic, you take whatever face the good doctor is offering. (If the dead wife isn't a bad-looking woman, all the better.) While recovering at his secluded estate, play along; let him call you "Eleanor" until you can walk out the front door on your own.

Any plastic surgeon can prune a nose, implant a chin, or iron out a few wrinkles around the eyes. If that's all you need, then open the Yellow Pages. But maybe you want more. Maybe you want to be six inches taller. Maybe you want blue eyes and a richer singing voice. Don't let any plastic surgeon dissuade you that such changes are beyond medicine. They're not. They are just beyond him, and you have way too much money not to find a far more gifted doctor.

The end of the Cold War has left unemployed true geniuses in plastic surgery, doctors who used to work for those now defunct foreign spy networks. That is good news for anyone seeking more than a simple little nip and tuck. These doctors can make you taller and change your eye color. If you want to be someone else—like that idiot blonde your man has fallen in love with—these surgeons are artists when it comes to creating impostors. They will not only give you the face you want, but the body type and the hair along with it. They will school you in the original's entire life history, then train you in all her mannerisms. When you're ready, they'll even make sure that the original isn't around to spoil your plans. By the time these doctors are through with you, even her own mother won't be able to tell the difference—and if she can, they'll take care of her, too.

Even when pressed for time, even when your boyfriend's face is on WANTED posters in every post office across the city, you can't just walk into any plastic surgeon's office for an emergency face-lift. Some plastic surgeons actually refuse to operate on known felons, not even for twice the money in the briefcase you're offering. Desperate, your boyfriend will probably do something stupid like taking the doctor and his nurse hostage. As the gun moll, it'll be your job to hold them at gunpoint while the doctor operates. Just don't hold out much hope of your boyfriend coming through this looking like Brad Pitt. When you unwrap the bandages a couple of weeks from now, you'll probably find nothing more than a nasty word carved into his forehead.

(Note: For any wanted felon who does manage to find a plastic surgeon who'll take your money—you won't be doing yourself any favors by getting the face of an even more wanted criminal than yourself.)

Medical professionals often broker deals with prisons to perform experimental surgery in exchange for reduced sentences or sometimes even full parole. If you're sitting in a prison for committing murder, this may be your best, your *only* chance of walking out the door. Yes, you do run a risk of disfigurement, but think positive! If the surgery is a success, you not only get your freedom, you get to go back and terrorize all your old enemies, who will have no idea who you are.

Plastic surgery is not an exact science. The results are not always permanent. A surgeon can give you a whole new face, one that ensures no one in town will recognize you, not even the lover who thought you died in that fire. A year or two down the line, you might very well look into a mirror and see your old face staring back at you. This, it should be noted, is not a gradual process. It happens with no warning. Whether or not anyone else notices this change, they will never mention it.

medical conditions you can fake

Pinching your nose and coughing into the phone may get you a day off from work, but it probably won't keep the police from arresting you for murder. When faced with such dilemmas, you need to learn how to fake something far more serious than the flu or a twisted ankle. You need to learn how to fake . . .

blindness

When a bomb explodes during the middle of posh fundraiser, someone is usually left blind from the concussion. They wake up in a brightly lit hospital room, asking why all the lights are off. Eventually, as the neurosurgeon promised, their eyesight is restored, but they don't feel the need to share that little miracle with anyone. When the doctor cannot find any medical reason why their sight hasn't returned, he will simply write the whole situation off as hysterical blindness.

Soap heroine and vixen alike have played this particular game of blind man's bluff, and so can you. Blindness allows you a distinct advantage for spying upon people. You have a much greater chance, for example, of catching your husband kissing his mistress on the terrace if neither one is worried about being seen. Blindness also allows you a catch-all excuse for being in all sorts of places you shouldn't be. What were you doing in the bushes underneath the balcony? You obviously got lost on your way down to the stables. During this time, when no one can hold any little accidents against you, spill a drink on your rival's brand new dress.

While you may not want to use the walking cane—the tap-tap-tapping on the ground will certainly alert people to your approach—you do need to wear the dark glasses. People like the suspicious other woman will be studying you, trying to determine whether you're staring blankly in her direction or really looking at her.

Avoid such scrutiny by hiding your eyes behind a very dark pair of sunglasses.

(Note: Hearing loss should never be attempted, not unless you've played Helen Keller on stage. Unlike blindness, it cannot be so easily faked. On the surface, it seems like a great way to trick people into talking freely in your presence. They certainly don't need to worry about some deaf girl eavesdropping on their plans, do they? Unfortunately, you won't have a prop like sunglasses to hide behind. If you react instinctively when someone calls your name, the game will be over.)

paralysis

If no one caught in the explosion has been blinded, temporarily or hysterically, then someone must have woken up in the hospital unable to feel their legs or move so much as a big toe. Maybe it wasn't an explosion. Maybe it was a car crash or a bullet to the spine during crossfire between mobs. As with the blindness, the effect is never permanent, and the patient tends to recover long before he or she ever reveals it to the rest of the town.

Before your injury, your husband was planning on leaving you for that other woman. Now, he wouldn't dare, not while you need him. (Note: Ironically, while a man will fake paralysis as a way of holding on to a woman, he would push that same woman he loves away if he were actually paralyzed.)

You hope that in caring for you and carrying you around the way he used to back when you were first married, your husband will fall in love with you again. But it won't happen overnight. Some nights, after he has tucked you safely into bed, he'll head out for a midnight rendezvous, unaware that you can follow. You will punish him for his indiscretion by letting him find you on the floor when he returns home. "Where were you?" you'll ask as he lifts you back into bed. "I was calling for you for hours." The guilt should keep him grounded at home for the foreseeable future.

At some point, your toddler will toddle into danger; she'll wander away from you and into a busy intersection. After a few seconds of screaming out ignored warnings, you are going to have to stand up and move. You're going to have to push your child out of the way of that speeding car. The moment you do, your husband will suddenly be standing there, behind your now empty wheelchair. You can claim that the emergency, the adrenaline rush has triggered a miracle recovery, but he'll soon realize that you've been able to walk for months. Then he'll do some walking of his own.

the unnamed but terminal illness

Your best friend, the man you were hoping would ask you to marry him one day, has fallen in love with your cousin. Before he can pop the question to her, you show up at his apartment in tears, needing a shoulder to cry on. You've just come from the doctor's, you tell him. You haven't told this to anyone, but you have been suffering from painful headaches for the last few months. The doctor ran some tests and the results just came in. You're dying. He's given you six months to live. Sympathetic, your friend asks if there's anything he can do. "Marry me," you say. "Till death do us part" doesn't sound so impossible to him, not when it's only a six-month commitment. Even your cousin is sympathetic and steps aside.

If you lie about having a specific illness, you have committed yourself to faking a very specific set of symptoms. That's why you need to keep the diagnosis mysterious as well as fatal.

When six months have come and gone and you're not dead yet, your husband is going to suspect that maybe

“Some nights, after he has tucked you safely into bed, he’ll head out for a midnight rendezvous, unaware that you can follow. You will punish him for his indiscretion by letting him find you on the floor when he returns home.”

you've conned him into this marriage. Plan ahead for this moment by mentioning at the outset that there is a slight chance of remission.

coma

At some point in your life, you will need to completely withdraw from the world. You don't want to face getting arrested for blackmail or the fallout from cheating on your husband with his own son. Maybe you just cannot testify against that mobster. In times like these, a coma offers a comfortable retreat, a chance to lie back and figure out your next move. If that next move requires eliminating a certain accountant who knows far too much for your own good, your coma offers an airtight alibi.

Be prepared for your disbelieving enemies coming into your hospital room with pins and needles to stick into your feet. Before beginning any sort of fake coma, you really need to study transcendental meditation.

amnesia

While a coma does offer a nice break from your current life, maybe you don't like to lie around doing nothing for weeks on end. Maybe you want to get out of town. Maybe you want to hop on the back of a motorcycle and take off for parts unknown. Maybe you want to meet somebody new; to kiss somebody besides your husband for a change, not forever, just for a little while. Amnesia gives you the freedom to do whatever you want without answering to another living soul.

While common on the soaps, amnesia isn't the easiest illness to contract, not if you don't want to go through getting hit on the head with a brick or suffer through some emotionally wrenching trauma first. But you can always just fake amnesia. Look at your husband one morning and ask, "Who are you?" When he asks you if you know your own name, shake your head in bewilderment. No, you don't know your own name, you have never seen your husband before, and "Where am I?" Sell that performance and your husband cannot blame you for anything you do next. You aren't yourself. (While you're not yourself, pick out a really cool new name.)

You really can't slip up with an amnesia ruse. If you accidentally call a friend by his name or head straight for the drawer where the matches are always kept, you've had a breakthrough. It doesn't mean that you're cured. It just means that you've taken a step toward regaining your memory. That memory doesn't need to come back *in toto* until you're good and ready to return to your old life.

split personality

Like faux amnesia, faking a split personality allows you to take a complete vacation from the life you're leading. You're no longer you. You are an alternate personality, a negative image of yourself. If you are prim and proper, your alter can be loud and trashy. If you can pull off acting so out of character, then you only need to work on your transitions from one personality to the next. Subtlety is the key here. Don't grab your head as though it were suddenly splitting apart; just tilt it to the side for a moment, close your eyes, then open them as if you are just waking up. You also cannot tell people that you have a second personality. They will only believe it if they figure it out on their own.

Unlike faux amnesia, from which you can recover rather quickly, faking a split personality comes with a hefty price tag: years and years of therapy. For that reason alone, a second personality should only be created in dire emergencies, like when you're on trial for a murder you actually did commit. If you can't pin the blame on anyone else, blame this alternate personality of yours. She was the one who held that pillow over the old man's face; you could never have done anything like that. The insanity defense will land you a short stay in a mental hospital, which is far preferable to life in prison.

heart attack

This ruse works best for people with an established history of cardiac problems. If you have already received a heart transplant, no one will dare doubt the sincerity of your attack.

At times, the walls will feel like they are closing in around you. Maybe the police are busting into your wedding shower with a warrant for your arrest, something about bribing public officials. Maybe your grandson has just discovered that you paid his trailer park fiancée to leave town. For one of the rare times in your life, you have not plotted out any contingency plans. Clutching your hand to your chest calls for an immediate time-out. The police interrogation will have to wait until after you've been checked out by a doctor. As for your grandson, he'll think twice before upsetting you over such trivial matters.

The great thing about the heart-clutch is that you can pull it out whenever you need it. Don't try it every day, but it is not limited to one time only. Even when people know that you're faking, they won't risk this being the one time you were telling the truth. (Somehow, an amoral vixen like you has managed to raise children with the capacity to feel guilt over causing a death.) Even your doctor can't claim that you were faking. He can tell them that you didn't have a heart attack, but he can't say for sure that the stress they all put you under didn't bring on chest pains.

miscarriage

Since you are probably faking your pregnancy to keep from losing your man to another woman, you need to engineer your own miscarriage. And you need to make it look as though this other woman caused it. The easiest way to accomplish this is to engage her in an argument at the top of a flight of stairs and make it look like she pushed you. Your husband's sympathy, coupled with his anger at the mistress who "killed his baby," should shift his devotion from her to you.

Make sure you choreograph this well. Improperly executed, this stunt could result in the mistress lying at the bottom of the stairs and you being accused of attempted murder.

childbirth

Any woman can fake a pregnancy, especially with those home kits. (See "Stocking the Medicine Cabinet.") Fooling a lab isn't even all that difficult. You just switch your blood sample with someone else's. Lab technicians, as you've undoubtedly noticed, are easily distracted and frequently called away. A soap heroine of your caliber can not only fake the home pregnancy kit and the lab test, she can continue the charade for nine months and then produce a real live baby.

To accomplish this, you will need a series of graduated stomach pads and one unwed mother. In a town like yours, the unwed mother should be easy to find. Scout out your obstetrician's waiting room for teens with that terrified look on their face. The stomach pads, by the way, can be ordered online.

You can work out a mutually beneficial relationship with the young mother-to-be: In exchange for this baby that she can't possibly keep, you will hide her from her boyfriend and her family. You can safely store her in your attic if it's properly ventilated. On top of taking this baby off her hands, you will give her lots and lots of money, enough to pay for college. It's a win-win solution for all parties involved.

Because of the padding, you do need to keep your husband at bay as well. Given the recent troubles in your marriage, he will be more than willing to oblige your request for separate bedrooms. He will blame your odd behavior—all those trips up to the attic in the middle of the night—on your hormones being out of whack.

As soon as the little mother goes into labor, you deliver the child and keep it. When your husband comes home from work, he will discover you cuddling the baby you've courageously given birth to on the living room floor. He will feel so horrible for not having been there when you needed him that he won't dig too deep into the particulars of how you delivered your own child.

The two of you will revel in the joys of parenthood up until the mother comes looking to get her baby back.

YOU KNOW YOU'VE BEEN MURDERED ON A SOAP IF . . .

✓ More than a dozen people have publicly threatened to murder you, all with good reason, in the last twenty-four hours.

✓ You've pointed at the killer and exclaimed, "You!" right before he pulled the trigger.

✓ Your glass of wine was poisoned at a masquerade ball.

✓ You have written a clue—not the name, mind you, just a clue—to your killer's identity with your own blood.

✓ No body was ever found, but someone was still sentenced to death by lethal injection.

the irascible millionaire's guide to estate planning

Once you have amassed your fortune through marriage and shady business deals, you need to think about drawing up your last will and testament. You do this for two reasons, neither of them a burning desire to share the wealth or to be remembered fondly:

1. You want to control your family from beyond the grave much as you did (or tried to do) while still alive.

2. You want to control that same cast of characters even more effectively during the waning years of your life. Nothing slaps a greedy relative into agreeable behavior better than the promise of

riches in the not-too-distant future or, even better, the unfathomable threat of disinheritance.

Some valuable tips for proper estate planning, the sort that will ensure complete control over your family both while you are living and after you head off to your own final reward . . .

- First and foremost, you need to retain a lawyer who specializes in estate planning, preferably a lawyer who is not sleeping with your daughter. While you undoubtedly have a law firm already representing you against the occasional murder accusation and frequent charges of political bribery, you will want an attorney whose sole priority is your will, as it will be changing from week to week, possibly even day to day, depending upon who has disobeyed you this time and what long-lost children have shown up on your doorstep.
- The fairest way to divvy up your estate would be to leave half to your husband, then divide up the other half equally among your children. Any lawyer who advises such action should be fired immediately and replaced by someone blessed with more creativity. A fair division of property

you could draw up yourself. It's simple math. A millionairess like you did not build the fortune you have with simple math—like paying a fair percentage of income tax, for example. You'll want a lawyer who enjoys drafting the unconscionable clauses and codicils you ask him to toss in. You want a lawyer whose glee in disinheriting heirs is second only to your own.

- It is very important to leave a respectable percentage of your estate to charity, preferably to a church with a large congregation. This part of the will must never be questioned or contested. After the sins you've committed to amass your fortune, you will need more than a few insincere mourners praying for your soul.
- There's a very good chance that your current husband has married you for your money. If this gigolo is younger than any of your children, it's probably closer to being an excellent chance. For being married to you for any length of time, he does deserve a sizable chunk of change, but not quite the chunk he feels he deserves. And there's no need to make the inheritance easy on him. He

undoubtedly loves the grand mansion you moved him into. He probably loves it more than he loves you. Since the legal system will not keep him from remarrying (that whole "till death do us part" loophole), you need to restrain him yourself. The house can be set up in a trust that will allow him to live there only until he remarries. Yes, he will be sleeping with other women along the way—he's probably begun doing so before you're even in the grave—but if he wants to keep the mansion, he will marry no other until the day he dies, which, for a healthy guy his age, is a long, long time.

- You can also tick off your husband by leaving a sizable fortune to your first ex. Let's face it, that man deserves it more than any of the others who have followed in his footsteps, more than all of them combined. He's the one who married you for you and then got dumped after it dawned on you the sort of rich husband your beauty could snare.

- As if you need to be told, your current spouse's children, the ones he had before you got married and the ones he fathered with other women while you were married, do not need to be heirs—unless you really want to tick off your biological children, who have been such disappointments you cannot believe they share your DNA.

- There is no reason why you can't have a little fun with your will. You are probably having a ball watching your relatives jump through hoops these last few months. Just because you're gone doesn't mean that the hoop-jumping needs to end. Instead of handing out bags of cash to people who think they've earned it, let them work a little harder for it. Since you will be leaving controlling interest in the family company to one heir, a contest might be the best way to judge who should be running that company. Perhaps you can leave each of the heirs/contestants a sum of money. Whoever parlays that sum into the greatest profit becomes CEO.

- You can devise any sort of contest you wish to award the grand prize, perhaps even the entire estate, to one sole winner. The contest should be something that will push the potential heirs to the limit, like being completely honest for an entire month, but nothing too crazy, like spending the

> "You can also tick off your husband by leaving a sizable fortune to your first ex."

night in a haunted house. That sort of codicil can be used to question your mental competency. You want your will to be a contest, not contested.

- Your competency must never come into question. You can never give your heirs (not that you can keep calling them that after you've cut them off) any ammunition to overturn your final final will. In addition to a lawyer, you should probably also keep a psychiatrist on retainer for weekly examinations. Best to schedule these examinations immediately before each will revision.
- Your will should also hold a few surprises. Death should not make you predictable. One way to shock everyone is to leave a sizable chunk of change, perhaps even controlling interest in your

company, to the least business-minded member of your family, the grandson who went surfing instead of to college. This will create lots of dissension among your family, especially with the grandson who holds an MBA from Wharton. The surfer grandson will keep imagining that you saw some great untapped potential in him, whereas the simple truth is this: You want the company to go under so nobody, especially the MBA, can ever claim he ran the business better than you.

- You can also manufacture shock at the will reading with a few well-planted red herrings. Your husband and your devious daughter, the one you think is sleeping with him, have already figured out the combination to your wall safe. So plant a fake will in there. While you won't be around to see it, you can imagine the looks on their faces when they walk into the lawyer's office, all smug and ready to collect their fortunes, only to find out that they're walking away with limited allowances that come with many, many strings.

- This will will also be your last chance to get rid of the gold-digging daughter-in-law who has seduced her way into your naïve youngest son's life. The young man doesn't receive one thin dime of your money until he gets a divorce. He will, of course, reject the money, opting instead for love. He's foolish that way, which is why any money left to him needs to be done so in a trust he cannot squander away on bird sanctuaries and homeless shelters. The daughter-in-law isn't quite so generous or willing to lead a simple life; she won't be sticking around for very long when she realizes that she's hitched her wagon to a falling star.

- You also might want to consider leaving a tidy sum of money to your lifelong enemy. The shock value alone will liven up the will reading. On a more practical note, in case there is any question of foul play in your demise (which there most likely will be), this will give the police the clear-cut motive they need to arrest him for your murder.
- The most important codicil to any will: The entire estate (all the money, the stocks, the properties . . . everything) reverts back to you the moment you return from the dead.

planning a truly memorable memorial . . .

Granted, a large percentage of the deaths on the soaps turn out to be false alarms: The presumed dead usually pops up in town a few years later, alive and well (save for the amnesia), making their funeral little more than a somewhat-sadder-than-average going-away party. Even so, you should never plan less than a truly memorable memorial service. Ninety percent of soap marriages don't last more than a year or two. That sad statistic hardly prevents you from planning a big, fancy wedding.

While a funeral rarely gives you as much time to prepare as a wedding, certain details cannot be overlooked:

The empty casket

A necessity since the body has never been recovered.

The oversized headshot, propped up on a tripod and surrounded by flowers

A simple framed picture on top of the coffin does not capture the grandeur of your late husband's life. (Just don't think too far in advance—like what, exactly, you are supposed to do with this poster after the ceremony.)

The press

The reporters and photographers do make getting into the service a bit more difficult, but your husband would be disappointed if his death didn't merit coverage by the local media and national tabloids.

The crying fit

Yes, it's a funeral, and there will be tears—presumably lots of tears. For one young woman, your step-daughter, the sadness of the occasion will be overwhelming. She will go running out of the service in tears. The young man who chases after her to see

"Assuming that your husband died under mysterious circumstances—and it's usually a safe assumption—the police like to make the first arrest during the memorial service."

if she is all right will inevitably end up comforting her with a long, meaningful kiss.

The drunken outburst

Midway through the service, your husband's illegitimate and alcoholic son will show up, whiskey in hand. Not that you'd need to see the bottle to know that he's been drinking. Don't worry about sliding down to make room. He won't be staying. He will insult the entire congregation of mourners, calling them hypocrites and claiming that he was the only one who ever really cared about his father.

The inappropriate mourner

This is separate from the drunken outburst, who had a legitimate right to show up, just not to show up drunk. A good example of the inappropriate mourner would be your late husband's mistress, the one whose bed he suffered his fatal heart attack in. In days of old, she would have hidden her face behind a thick black veil and slid into the back pew; maybe she would have watched from the alcove. These days, she shows up in a black dress with the sort of plunging neckline that brought on the fatal heart attack. Her arrival will be met with a buzz of questions: "What's *she* doing here?" Of course, you will confront her to let her know in no uncertain terms, "You don't belong here." The mistress will retort, "I have every right to be here. I loved him too—and he loved me." She will, however, cede you the front pew.

The song

At least one of your close personal friends was born with a remarkable singing voice. She may not sing professionally at the local nightclub—she may be the assistant district attorney—but her voice

> "Midway through the service, your husband's illegitimate and alcoholic son will show up, whiskey in hand."

belongs on Broadway. Under the circumstances, you can coax her into a song, which will either be "Amazing Grace" or some melancholy but current Top Forty hit.

The telegrams

More surprising than those virtual strangers who show up at a funeral are the notable absentees. Few, if any, of your husband's friends and relatives who have moved away will come back to town. Even his own mother might stay away, unable to watch her only son get buried. These absences will be explained away with a litany of telegrams, bearing weak excuses which are not to be questioned on such a sad occasion: unreachable by phone; an inner ear infection that prevents air travel; et cetera, et cetera.

The arrest

Assuming that your husband died under mysterious circumstances—and it's usually a safe assumption—the police like to make the first arrest during the memorial service. Of course, etiquette dictates that such an arrest wait until the end of the service. If possible, the arrest should be made by one of the mourners.

the best places to stage your return from the dead

You have gone to an awful lot of troubling faking your own death. You paid off a string of hospital technicians to rewire your heart and brain monitors. You gave the coroner a small fortune to declare you dead and the mortician another kingly sum to dupe up a corpse to look like you. Now that you've accomplished your secret mission, the one everybody needed to think you were dead for, you're getting homesick. You miss your husband. You miss your kids. You even miss your enemies. But you can't just let yourself into your house and be waiting on the couch when the family gets home. You could, but come on. You put so much effort into your death, you need to put an equal effort into your return from the dead.

Some tips on where to stage your Return from the Dead . . .

your own funeral

Who hasn't daydreamed about popping up at his own funeral to see who showed, who didn't, and who's crying? Walking in mid-service gives you the chance to do something you've only done at weddings—object. With emotions already running high, that kind of return is guaranteed at least one fainter.

The trouble with coming back for your own funeral . . . it doesn't give you much time to play dead. Your return will be dramatic, but not one fraction as much as it could be if you've been presumed dead for a year or two. If you absolutely have to see your funeral, you can spy on the proceedings from the choir loft.

your own grave

Of course, you will visit your grave at night, preferably on a foggy evening. Pick a special date (your birthday, the first anniversary of your "death," one of your wedding anniversaries, perhaps), basically any day that your husband will be bringing flowers by. When he sees you through the fog and says, "Excuse me," you can turn around slowly to reveal yourself. But only for a second. You must then disappear into the fog. For the next few weeks, he'll be walking around town, convinced that you are still alive, while all his friends try to convince him that you were just some hallucination caused by a combination of the fog and his lingering grief.

the trial for your murder

Yes, the bomb that blew your cabin into toothpicks had been planted to do the same to you. That gives you more than enough reason to head into hiding, not letting even your nearest and dearest know that you survived the blast. As long as your would-be killer (whoever that really is) thinks that he's done you in, he won't be looking to try again. Once the guilty party is arrested and put on trial, you may decide to reveal yourself. Yes, this will help him beat the murder rap, but now that you know who's to blame, you can dish out a whole lot better revenge than any judge. That doesn't mean you shouldn't let your would-be killer sweat out his fate. Wait until just before the verdict is read to walk into the courtroom. With so many news reporters already in there, you couldn't maximize the press coverage if you owned the TV station and the newspaper. (Wait a minute, you do own both. That's why your son-in-law wanted you dead.)

at the execution

If you really want to string out the tension and make your "killer" sweat, you can wait until the night of the execution to come out of hiding. You can while away the days in some European castle while your "killer" counts down his final days inside a prison cell. Unless you want to see him executed for a crime he didn't quite commit, which he would definitely deserve, leave yourself enough time to sneak past the prison guards at the gate. You want to pop up alive in those seconds after the lethal injection has been given but before it has reached the vein. At that moment, even your worst enemy (at least, the only one who's tried to kill you so far) will be glad to see you alive and well.

your husband's wedding

You can't really blame your husband for moving on after your death. You may not be thrilled with his choice of wife, but you waived your right to any say in that decision the day after your funeral. Try to get to the church before any vows are exchanged. You might make a splashier entrance catching the bouquet at the reception, but by that time he's legally another woman's husband. The marriage cannot be invalidated while you're still legally dead. And do you really want to see your husband married to anyone—even if it's only for a day?

at a masquerade ball

These galas with their masks on a stick and lavishly decorated costumes are just begging for a dramatic surprise or two. (When people get dressed for Halloween, they expect either a trick or a treat.) The right costume will allow you to mingle about the room for a few hours, spying on your family and friends, catching up on their lives via the local gossip. You will, of course, wait until the unmasking to reveal yourself. What better climax to an evening of mystery than for you to herald your return from the great beyond. Just make sure you're the last one to reveal yourself because you don't want the shocked looks on everyone's faces covered up by papier-mâché.

your own surprise party

Although etiquette frowns upon people throwing parties for themselves, you can hardly expect anyone to throw you a party if you've been dead for the past few years. You need to send out invitations to everyone with whom you had dealings—good, bad, and sexual—before you "died." A nice buzz will build around this upcoming soiree: Who is this mystery host? Why have we all been invited? During the course of the evening, when that interest has reached its peak, you will emerge, preferably onto a stage. Before the party, check out the acoustics to determine the best spot from which to hear every last gasp.

the soap heroine personality quiz

If you intend to lead a soapier life, you need to figure out exactly into which category you fit. Depending upon your age and level of naïveté, you might qualify as an ingénue, in which case the future is still open to you. Maybe you're the long-suffering heroine, the one always being cheated on and widowed. If this is the case, you can't be out there stealing other women's husbands. That's a job for the town vixen, who may or may not also double as the diva. While you will undoubtedly be taken hostage from time to time, you'll need to leave the actual crime-fighting to the adventuress. Figure out what you are quickly, before the roles are filled. You don't want to end up the psycho—or worse, the best friend with great advice but no storyline of her own.

1. How many times do you expect to get married in the course of your lifetime?
   - **a.** Not more than ten.
   - **b.** Once. True love lasts forever.
   - **c.** Three. The first time for money. The second time to wake up the man I love and make him realize how much he wants me. The third time should be the one that takes.
   - **d.** First off, you really can't count the marriage if the groom was shot dead before we left the church.
   - **e.** Just one more time, and I'll sit here in my wedding dress until he shows up.

2. How many children do you plan on having?
   - **a.** Between the ones I give birth to, the ones I adopt, my husband's children from his first wife, and the street kid I take in, at least half a dozen.
   - **b.** None before I'm married.

> Depending upon your age and level of naïveté, you might qualify as an ingénue, in which case the future is still open to you.

c. Two, unless they're easily manipulated, in which case I can handle a third.

d. Babies slow you down in the jungle.

e. This rag doll I can sing lullabies to is baby enough for me.

3. What keeps you up at night?

a. Worries about my children. They get into so much trouble. Also, this hacking cough that won't go away.

b. My boyfriend. When he calls to say good night, I just can't say good-bye.

c. My lover. And occasionally my lover's wife banging at my door, looking for him.

d. Searching for the man who shot my boyfriend.

e. My alternate personalities.

4. What is your dream job?

a. Nursing at the same hospital where my husband is a respected surgeon.

b. A runway model or a singer. Maybe both.

c. Head of my own cosmetics empire.

d. Spy.

e. Advice columnist.

5. What does Christmas mean to you?

a. One day without anyone in my family being kidnapped, shot, or diagnosed with something fatal.

b. I think my boyfriend is giving me an engagement ring.

c. Another day my lover will be stuck at home with that insufferable wife of his.

d. The perfect opportunity to search a suspect's home while he's at Midnight Mass.

e. A forty-eight-hour pass from the asylum to wreak all the havoc I can.

6. Your brother has just discovered that he is not biologically related to your family. What is your first reaction?

a. He needs to know that, DNA or not, he's still a member of this family; he will always be my brother.

b. If we're not related, then there's no reason why we can't date, is there?

c. More inheritance for me.

d. Someone switched those babies, and I'm going to find out who.

e. No response, just a catatonic rocking back and forth.

7. If you caught your husband in bed with another woman, how would you respond?

a. I guess I'd file for divorce again.

b. He would never do that to me.

c. That would give me carte blanche to pursue a relationship with his business partner. Actually, to pursue it openly.

d. I'd be on the next plane heading to anyplace but here.

e. That depends. If the bed heets are flame retardant, I'll have to resort to plan **b.**

8. Which would disturb you most to find out about your groom's first wife?

a. Legally, she's still married to him.

b. He's still in love with her.

c. She looks exactly like me.

d. She died under very suspicious circumstances.

e. She survived the car accident.

9. What do you consider your proudest moment in life?

a. Becoming a mother.

b. Winning that beauty pageant.

c. Taking over my mother's business and then stealing her husband.

d. Bringing down the crime family that ordered the hit on my fiancé.

e. Convincing a whole panel of psychiatrists that I was sane enough to be set free on my old enemies.

10. The doctor has just told you that you have six months to live. How will you spend your remaining days?

a. Hiding the truth from my husband and children. They don't need to know until the night before I die, at which point I will gather them all together for a family dinner.

b. Getting married to my boyfriend and making every last moment with him count.

c. The first five months, I'd track down all my favorite ex-lovers for one final fling with each. That last month, I suppose I should make a few amends.

d. Scouring the rain forests for that rare plant which is the essential ingredient in a miracle cure.

e. Plotting my own murder, so I can frame my husband's mistress for the crime.

decoding your answers

If the majority of your answers are (a), stock up on the tissues, because you're the long-suffering heroine. Since countless medical crises will be headed your way, make sure that your health insurance is up to date.

If the majority of your answers are (b), you are the ingénue, full of hope and romantic dreams. Don't worry, you'll grow out of it pretty quickly—like right after you catch your boyfriend in bed with another girl.

If the majority of your answers are (c), that makes you the vixen. Of course, that works on the presumption that you've answered these questions honestly—and when is the last time you did something like that?

If the majority of your answers are (d), you are the adventuress. It's surprising that you could find time in your schedule to take this quiz. You must be on a stakeout.

If you answered (e) to any of the questions—and don't go nuts or nuttier when you read this—you are the psycho. Seriously, put down the letter opener.